Eyes Wide Open

...when life happens you want to see it coming!

Every day is an adventure! I hope you enjoy the stories.

Robin

March 2012

Eyes Wide Open

Copyright © 2011 by R. K. Livingston.

All rights reserved. No part of this book may be used or reproduced in any manner whatsoever without written permission from the publisher except in the case of brief quotations embodied in critical articles and reviews.

Published by Lulu.com

ISBN: 978-1-257-95805-4

Cover design © 2011 by R. K. Livingston

All photographs and personal names used by permission.

Scripture quotation taken from the Holy Bible, New Living Translation, copyright © 1996. Used by permission of Tyndale House Publishers, Inc., Wheaton, Illinois 60189. All rights reserved.

To my family, both here and gone, whose stories have made my life a feast.

To my friend, Nikki, who encouraged me to write them down.

Eyes Wide Open

****

The soft summer air is alive with birdsong as I drag another chair out to add to the mismatched allotment already scattered on the back deck of my brother's house. The sun feels warm on my upturned face as I settle in with the first coffee of the day.

It's early but most of us don't care much for sleeping in anyway. Already the talk is animated and punctuated with laughter as jokes and comments are tossed back and forth among the family members gathered here. I started out with three brothers but once you add in our spouses and the next generation or two, we make quite a crowd.

One thing leads to another as it inevitably does whenever two or more of us are in one place. The talk turns to the past…adventures shared…disasters survived…all the follies and fun of lives well lived.

"There's a story in that," someone shouts on hearing a veiled reference to the dangers of canoe camping. "Let's hear it!"

My brother, Richard, is happy to oblige and launches into a lively account of his worst ever camping trip and its unexpected pitfalls. Cups are set aside and

Eyes Wide Open

people lean forward in their seats, eyes alight and smiles twitching at the corners of mouths. We know how it will end. We've heard it before but it loses nothing in the retelling.

My gaze wanders from face to face, this family of mine sitting rapt as Richard leaps to his feet, waving his arms with a flourish to illustrate a point. I can't help but notice the faces that are missing. Mom and Dad, gone now but always looming large in our hearts, loved these get-togethers. In my mind's eye they are still here, sitting proud and content in the midst of their children and grandchildren. I can hear my mother's laughter ringing out with the rest as Richard reaches the hilarious climax of his tale of woe.

I think of other gatherings, earlier times, when we were all younger and still looking ahead to much of our lives. Mom and Dad had stories of their own to tell and we never got tired of hearing them. So many of those stories are lost now, remembered only in bits and pieces like imperfect glimpses into a past that is gone. Only the best loved and most often repeated remain to be dragged out and shared at family reunions like this one.

One day even those will be gone. Somebody really ought to write them down. Hmmm...why not?

****

Eyes Wide Open

Small but Mighty

My dad's family spent a number of years attempting to farm on land just north of Alban, Ontario. Of course farming up there was a bit of a mixed bag that no one actually made a living at. One day his father came home with what sounded like an irate chicken in a burlap bag. He dropped the sack in the yard and its occupant struggled free of the muffling folds to take stock of its new surroundings. It was a little Banty rooster, only a quarter the size of the rooster the farm already had.

No mention was made of why there was any need for a second rooster on the place, especially one as diminutive as this one was. He would have ended up in the stewpot that very day if Grandma had had her way but Grandpa wouldn't hear of it. I've often wondered if he might have won him in a bet but dismissed it as unlikely in that strictly Catholic household.

Banty roosters were used in cockfighting and were known for their aggressive nature. This one was no exception. When the farm's rooster crowed at sunrise the next morning the little Banty considered it a personal challenge and rushed to the attack. Dust and feathers flew and the short but intense battle ended with the farm's rooster in full retreat.

Within two days the larger bird was a silent and tattered version of his former self. He had learned that crowing of any sort would inevitably result in a sound

Eyes Wide Open

thrashing by his tiny arch nemesis and the little Banty had become the undisputed "King of the Barnyard".

When the Banty turned up missing soon after that there was a lot of speculation among the children about various forms of rooster revenge until someone recalled that the morning had been particularly still and they had heard the crowing of the neighbor's rooster from the farm a mile up the road. It seemed unlikely but they decided it might be worth checking. Sure enough, within a half a mile or so they caught up to the little Banty strutting up the middle of the road, head up and feathers all puffed out, clearly making his way to face off with whichever rooster he'd heard daring to crow that morning.

That little rooster was more trouble than he was worth but Grandpa seemed to like him a lot. I think he probably felt a certain kinship with the scrappy bird. My Grandpa Landry wasn't very big either. When I knew him he still walked with a spring in his step, shoulders back and chin thrust out. Most often I would see him with a twinkle in his blue eyes and a ready smile but I've been told he was quite a scrapper in his younger years.

He had ambitions to become a boxer and actually fought in a few matches. He was quick and strong but he couldn't manage to keep a cool head in a fight. His temper would inevitably get the best of him and ultimately it spoiled his chances of being competitive in the ring. Even so, he never could back down from anything. It was a quality he and the rooster shared. They never thought of

Eyes Wide Open

themselves as small and that just might be worth remembering when I face the Goliaths in my own life.

Eyes Wide Open

Would You Like That With Mayo?

When I was in High School we lived on the Espanola turn-off right next to an Esso gas station that had a little restaurant attached. We ran the restaurant for one summer and the whole family had to get involved. My dad was still working in the mines so his contribution was to sit in the back room from time to time peeling potatoes. My mom was the one with experience so she taught the rest of us how to wait on tables, operate a cash register, and cook in a short order kitchen. She and my oldest brother, Richard, ran the day shift and my next oldest brother, Dave, and I ran the evening shift. Of course, if a busload of tourists or hockey players pulled up we could just pick up the phone and call next door for reinforcements.

It wasn't a very big place but when it filled up things were hopping. That was the case one evening when Dave and I were on the job. The grill was sizzling and there was a buzz of conversation as I made my way briskly from booth to booth. We were definitely in our groove and everything was operating like a well oiled machine. Dave had several plates all lined up and ready to load in the kitchen with fish and chips in the fryer and burgers cooking on the grill. He was building a couple of club sandwiches when he reached under the counter for the gallon jug of mayonnaise we kept there.

What I heard was a heavy hollow sounding thump followed by an inarticulate bellow. All conversation ceased

Eyes Wide Open

and I rushed into the kitchen with visions of severed fingers lending speed to my feet. What greeted my eyes was not nearly as lurid as what my vivid imagination had conjured up in those few seconds of panic. Even so it was bad enough...so bad in fact that I couldn't stop myself sagging against the doorframe, completely overcome by the irresistible urge to laugh out loud.

Dave stood immobile in the centre of the kitchen with the empty mayonnaise jug on the floor at his feet, its lid still clutched in one hand. He was almost entirely covered in a thick coating of mayo. In fact the whole kitchen, which wasn't very large, was covered in mayo. There were even splatters on the ceiling. He had grabbed the jug by the lid and swung it around and up to set it on the counter when the lid let go in mid swing. The jug hit the floor squarely and with some force but because it was plastic it didn't break. Instead the entire gallon of mayonnaise was forcefully ejected out of its mouth like grape-shot out of a cannon aimed at the moon - physics in real life.

Dave slowly removed his glasses revealing two perfectly round patches of clear skin around his eyes. He grinned, teeth white in a white face. "I think we'd better call for reinforcements," he conceded as he groped for the nearest towel.

Fortunately none of our customers was in a hurry. When Dave emerged from the kitchen to sweep off his cap and take a bow they thought the entertainment well worth the delay.

Eyes Wide Open

Never Shop Alone

I've never been fond of shopping. Crowds…noise…struggling in and out of outfits that look better on a hanger than on me…prices that seem totally outrageous to my untrained eye…sore feet…frustration…discouragement. What it all boils down to is that when I do find something I like, I generally wear it for at least 10 years just to avoid going through the whole process again.

There was a time when I looked on shopping as a solo occupation, an unpleasant task to be gotten over with as quickly as possible. That all changed the day I was forced to go looking for a new summer dress a few years back. I started in a very large department store which shall remain nameless since I don't remember its name.

I pushed through the door to the dressing room area with one hip, encumbered as I was with purse and an armload of possibilities that gave me some slight hope that I might find something in my first attempt. I was faced with a choice of cubicles, each with a door that left about 8 inches open at top and bottom. None of them were in use at the time so I made sure I chose one with a lock that actually worked. The process of trying on clothes is fraught with enough anxiety without adding the stress of worrying that someone might pull the door open on you standing there in your 10 year old second best underwear.

Eyes Wide Open

I tried on each of the five dresses I carried in with me. Four were definitely going back on the hangers but the fifth had potential. I silently weighed the chances of me finding something better and in the end decided I would take it. I was actually smiling as I reached for the door handle. The smile crumpled in on itself when the handle wouldn't budge. I dropped everything and tried with both hands. I tried with the little lock button pushed to the left. I tried with it pushed to the right. I rattled it and shook it and banged it with the heel of my hand all to no avail.

I was alone in the dressing room area or someone surely would have responded to all the noise I was making. I rested my forehead against the door, tears of frustration welling up in my eyes. This just couldn't be happening to me. I glanced down at the opening under the door and briefly entertained the idea of trying to squeeze through it. Had I been a 12 year old it might even have worked. As it was I was just going to have to wait it out.

After what seemed like hours the outer door opened and I heard the footsteps of some other hopeful shopper approaching.

"Excuse me…Hello? Somebody? Anybody?" My voice sounded ragged even to my own ears. "Can you please go and tell someone from the store that I'm stuck in here? I can't get the door open."

Whoever it was didn't respond but the rapidly retreating footsteps and the noise of the outer door swinging

Eyes Wide Open

shut left me at least a little hopeful. That hope was beginning to evaporate as the minutes ticked by.

Eventually, my straining ears were rewarded and a brisk male voice called out, "Maintenance here".

I sighed in relief as he set to work unscrewing the hinges on the door to remove it. In moments it was done. I barely glanced at his grinning face as he replaced the screwdriver in the tool belt at his waist. I couldn't get out of there fast enough to suit me. I was all the way home before I realized I'd left the dress I meant to buy in the dressing room, totally forgotten in my haste to escape.

"Aaargh!" I was going to have to go back….maybe in about 10 years. Next time I'd bring someone along for back up.

Eyes Wide Open

Bears in the Berry Patch

The raspberries are ripe and it's time to pick. These days I only have to step around to the back of our garage to get our fill of the luscious fruit. Where's the adventure in that? When I was growing up in Northern Ontario, the berries we picked were growing wild. Getting in a supply for the pies and preserves my mother made was one of summer's major undertakings. As soon as we could walk we were drafted into the family picking brigade. Off we would go with as many plastic pails and baskets as we could carry and there was no quitting until every last one was full or the berries ran out.

Strawberries were always first. Wild strawberries grow in open fields and we would end up on some abandoned farm on a dusty back road where the grass grew tall and the only sound was the buzz of cicadas in the summer heat. I never knew a strawberry could grow bigger than the size of a pea until we moved to Southern Ontario.

The enormous strawberries grown on farms down here may be easier to pick but they just don't taste the same. Maybe the hours we spent on our knees in the grass with the hot sun baking our skin and squadrons of deer flies circling our heads like winged halos lent extra flavor to the fruit. The promise of that first bowl of strawberries and whipped cream was the ultimate reward my mother would dangle in front of us to silence our complaints.

Eyes Wide Open

Blueberries were much easier to pick. They grew on rocky hills where you could always find a bit of shade. We would spread out and compete to find the best patch, preferably one where you could sit in the middle reaching in every direction to pick with both hands. My brother, Tom, and I would check in with each other now and then to see who was winning in the race to fill our pails. If the picking was good my mother would want us to fill our hats as well. It sometimes took more than one trip to get it all to the car.

Raspberries came last in the season and they were my favorite. We would usually end up covered in scratches but at least we could pick standing up. On one momentous day we hiked through the bush to reach an abandoned gravel pit where the raspberries grew wild. It didn't take long for us to scatter. Competition is a great motivator. My mother was completely focused on the task at hand and she didn't pay much attention to where Tom and I went. By then we were seasoned pickers and able to fend for ourselves. Consequently, we were nowhere near her when she got the surprise of her life.

She was leaning forward using both hands to deftly pluck the fruit from the prickly branches when she heard a rustling on the far side of the bush she was working on. She assumed it was one of us and paid little attention. She straightened up to move to a new spot at the precise moment a black bear that had been gorging itself on the late summer fruit opposite her also rose. For a split second they stared at each other from a distance of only a few feet but my mother's paralysis didn't last long. The peaceful solitude of the clearing was shattered as she screamed and

Eyes Wide Open

scrambled backwards, berries flying in all directions. The bear let out a great "Humph" and dropped to all fours to run for the shelter of the trees as fast as its legs could carry it. I think my mother scared it half to death. A scream from her could have that effect.

Unfortunately, it ran directly into the trees that we would have to pass through to reach the car. Picking was over for that day. We stayed only long enough to give the bear a good head start and then we began our march making as much noise as we possibly could. I'm sure the bear was long gone but even so we set a new record for the number of times we sang "Row, Row, Row Your Boat" at the top of our lungs as we stomped through the brush. I think the lyrics should have been changed to "Bear's in the berry patch. What are we to do? Scream and shout and jump about, and he'll be scared of you."

Eyes Wide Open

Flap That Dress

I've always prided myself on being a quick learner so when my husband, Bev, asked me if I thought I could handle being a farm wife I rose to the challenge. He got a job as a Dairy Herdsman and we moved to the country. I must admit I felt a little intimidated by the cows at first. In time I began to feel more confident though, especially when they were lined up neatly and safely locked into the stanchions. They were so placid and well behaved. That was before the fateful Sunday we met under very different circumstances.

We pulled into our lane after a particularly grueling church service. Being nearly eight months pregnant made almost everything grueling back then. I wanted nothing more than a nap at that moment. In fact I had already closed my eyes when I heard Bev's explosive "Oh no!" and felt the car lurch to a sudden standstill.

There in the yard ahead of us was a group of at least a dozen escapees from the adjoining pasture. It seemed to me that there were cows everywhere. Bev reacted quickly. He maneuvered the car into a position that would block the lane and got out to confront the miscreants. In a series of fits and starts I managed to gain the house where I watched nervously from the safe haven of the porch.

Perhaps they didn't recognize the suit and tie or perhaps their first taste of freedom had gone to their heads but those cows were being particularly uncooperative.

Eyes Wide Open

Time and time again he would get them started in the right direction and they would scatter as they approached the gate. Finally, he called out to me that I would have to help.

"I can't chase cows in my condition!" I shouted in instant apprehension.

"You don't have to chase them," he responded patiently. "Just put on some boots and come out here."

This crisis was obviously going to require teamwork so I reluctantly made my way out to the yard feeling clumsy and awkward in oversized boots.

"What do I do?" I asked.

"I want you to go through the gate and out into the field, say about a hundred yards or so," Bev explained, pointing over the fence to the pasture the cows seemed so determined to avoid.

"Then what?" I wondered.

"Just flap your dress," he instructed with a nod of encouragement.

"Flap my dress?" I looked down at myself in bewilderment. The red dress I was wearing looked more like a tent than anything else and I couldn't figure out what he was getting at. It sounded a lot easier than chasing cows though, so I waddled out into the empty field and took up my position.

Eyes Wide Open

If I had known the likely result of such a display, I probably would not have flapped that dress with such naïve abandon. One by one heads lifted and turned in my direction. The nearest cow, its curiosity peaked, took a few tentative steps toward the gate. The next thing I knew, what looked like a full scale stampede was on and it was coming straight at me.

I froze in mid flap, rooted to the spot in horrified expectation of a fatal trampling. The charge lasted only seconds but I could have sworn it was much longer. To my utter amazement, those cows came to an abrupt stop within feet of where I stood. I reminded myself to resume breathing as I looked into several pairs of huge brown eyes and searched for signs of aggression. However, not even my overactive imagination could turn milk cows into anything but milk cows.

As I stood there trying to anticipate their next move, they lost interest in me and began to wander and graze as if nothing had happened. It seemed a rather flat ending to my 'near death' experience.

I trudged back to my grinning husband who shouted, "Well done!" as he latched the gate. He obviously knew I had never been in the slightest danger.

"All in a day's work," I responded with a shaky smile.

Eyes Wide Open

Up the Creek

My Mom and Dad loved fishing. They kept it up long after my Dad gave up hunting. Eventually, they reached an age where putting a boat or canoe in the water was too much for them so they had to content themselves with fishing from the shore. Unfortunately, most of the lakes with easy access were pretty much fished out so there wasn't much excitement in it.

Dad remembered a lake in the French River area that was quite a ways off the beaten track. He knew they were much more likely to succeed in catching something there so one morning they set out to find it, trusting to Dad's memory and sense of direction to get them where they were going.

It all started out well. Dad easily located the narrow back road that would ultimately take them to the vicinity of the lake. It was a bit rough but he was an excellent driver and he had no trouble negotiating the ruts and potholes they encountered. It wasn't the first time he'd taken their Chrysler Dynasty over roads that looked more like cow paths. The trouble started when they came to a creek where the bridge had washed out. Actually it was more like a river. It didn't look to be very deep but it was more than three car lengths across.

They were faced with a choice. There was no room to turn around so if they decided to abandon their plan they would have to back all the way out to the main road which

Eyes Wide Open

was only given that distinction because it allowed for two way traffic. The prospect didn't appeal to either of them especially with no fish to show for their efforts. Dad got out for a closer inspection of the bank. There he could plainly discern the tire tracks of another vehicle leading straight into the water. When he looked to the other side, the tracks leading up the far bank and onto the road were easily visible. That settled it. If some other driver had made it across there was no reason he couldn't do it too.

Mom was a nervous passenger at the best of times so I can well imagine her white knuckled grip on the dashboard as Dad put the car in first gear and drove into the water. What he didn't know of course was that whoever had driven across ahead of him was most certainly not doing it in a Chrysler. Even so, they made it right out to the centre before the wheels sank deep in the loose gravel of the riverbed and they came to a shuddering halt. They were well and truly stuck and no amount of skill was going to get them out of this one. There they sat, neither one willing to look at the other, water seeping in around the doors until it covered the floorboards and sloshed around their ankles.

Who knows how long they might have sat there if not for the return of the vehicle whose tracks they had been following. It turned out to be two men in a 4x4 Jeep with a convenient winch on the front. Those men must have wondered if they were seeing things. After all, what are the odds that you could pull up to the bank of a river in the middle of nowhere and encounter two very senior citizens parked in midstream? Yet there they sat in tight-lipped silence in the front seat of their car while the river flowed

Eyes Wide Open

around them. I'm quite sure the men in the jeep had never before seen two unlikelier off-road enthusiasts. Fortunately for my Dad's injured pride, they managed not to laugh once as they set about rescuing the stranded couple.

I can't say the same for the rest of us when we heard the story. Of course by then even my Dad was ready to see the humor in it. The trip may not have netted them any fish but it was an adventure all right. Even senior citizens need one of those from time to time.

Eyes Wide Open

Gotcha!

I am often lost in a world of daydreams and when that is the case it can be fairly easy to startle me. When Bev and I were dating and then on into the first year of our marriage he thought it highly amusing to jump out at me from darkened doorways or creep up on me from behind. He could always count on a pretty dramatic reaction and the more I bristled with righteous indignation, the more hilarious he found it.

We'd been married nearly a year and were living in Prospect Heights, Illinois studying Missions with the aim of going overseas. We shared a large house with a number of other students and teammates. Our upstairs bedroom had an ensuite bathroom and Bev had gone up to get a shower when I decided it was time for some payback at last.

I crept up the stairs, stealthy footsteps muffled by the thick carpet in the hall. If I leaned to my right I could just see into the room without exposing my position. The bathroom door was closed and I could hear the reassuring sound of water running. There was a wall to wall closet with sliding doors just inside the doorway on the right so I carefully began to ease the slider open, checking over my shoulder every few seconds to make sure he was still in the bathroom. Oh, revenge was going to be so sweet.

I backed into the closet doing my best not to disturb the hangers or make the slightest noise that would give me away. Bev had notoriously good hearing. I could hardly

Eyes Wide Open

restrain my gleeful anticipation as I slid the door across inch by careful inch to conceal my hiding place. With only the last couple of inches to go the gloom in the tight confines of the closet was almost complete. I turned my head and nearly jumped out of my skin. He was supposed to be in the shower but there he was in the dimness only inches from me, his grinning face barely discernable as he peered at me from where he'd been struggling to hold his breath as he waited concealed among the coats.

I can't imagine what the people downstairs thought when they heard the piercing shriek followed by a scuffle and a tremendous crash coming from our bedroom. In my frantic efforts to get out of that closet I knocked the sliding door completely off its track and it went down like a felled tree with me on top of it. By the time our housemates thundered up the stairs and burst in to see what happened we were both sitting on the floor laughing so hard that tears were rolling unrestrained down our cheeks and we were gasping for air.

"I almost need resuscitating," I finally managed, my heart beating against my ribs like a trapped bird.

Bev had to admit that he'd been pretty startled himself when the closet door started to slide open seemingly of its own accord. It took everything in him to keep silent when he realized what I was doing. It ended up being the last prank of its kind for either one of us. There's a limit to what closet doors and hearts can take.

Eyes Wide Open

Wait Till You See What I Did

My parents lived on a farm on the highway between Alban and Noelville in Northern Ontario when they were in their twenties. Dad would go out to work for the Department of Highways during the day and attend to all the farm work in the evenings and on the weekends. When Friday night rolled around Mom was always hopeful that they might be able to go out for some fun but Dad was often just too tired.

House parties were the favorite form of social gathering back then. People would take turns hosting. Furniture would be pushed aside to make room for dancing with fiddles, harmonicas, and guitars providing the music. A late night lunch made up of a washtub full of sandwiches was all that was needed to round off the evening.

One day Mom decided that if she could do some of Dad's farm work while he was away he might be willing to take her out on Friday night. She knew there were some cut logs back in the bush that he had been meaning to haul to the house so they could be cut and split for firewood. The horse would be doing all the hauling so she was confident she could handle the job. She kept silent about her plans as Dad headed off to work in the morning. This was going to be her gift to him, a total surprise, and she could hardly wait to get started. The moment he pulled out of the driveway she was scrambling into some old work clothes and slipping into her rubber boots.

Eyes Wide Open

      She had never actually harnessed the horse before but figured she had a basic idea of what to do. It took a while but eventually she got the collar fitted and all the straps and buckles securely fastened. Her step was confident as she led the horse to the back of the farm and onto the rutted track that led into the bush. She worked hard that day. It wasn't easy getting the chain around the logs so they wouldn't slip. One at a time seemed the best course of action. Each one was a struggle though, and she had to resort to what amounted to an undignified wrestling match with the bigger logs that left her sweating and covered in mud.

      It was much harder than she'd dreamed and even the horse seemed determined to thwart her. Every now and then he would set his feet stubbornly and refuse to move unless she gave him a good smack. The hours dragged by and the unlikely duo made trip after trip with dogged determination until they were finally on the last load and Mom was beginning to feel a sense of smug self satisfaction. They emerged from the trees to see Dad standing in the yard staring at the pile of logs no doubt wondering what on earth was going on. Mom's weariness seemed to evaporate and she strode forward proudly, struggling unsuccessfully to suppress her triumphant grin as he turned and spotted her coming. Seeing his incredulous stare when he met them at the edge of the yard made it all worthwhile.

      "You did all this?" he asked, his forehead furrowed in concern as his gaze wavered between her and the horse. "You've been pulling logs all day?"

Eyes Wide Open

"Of course," Mom responded with pride. "I'm stronger than you think."

Her elation evaporated when he shook his head and explained that she had the horse collar on upside down. He thought it should have been obvious that the narrow part of the teardrop shaped horse collar was meant for the back of the horse's neck. That was the only way he could pull without choking. It wasn't obvious to Mom though. She had taken one look at the collar and put it on the way she would have worn it herself…with the narrow part in front.

"Good thing you were only pulling one log at a time or you might have strangled him," Dad pronounced as he set about releasing the poor beast.

It was a pretty flat ending to Mom's ambitious plan to surprise and impress her hard-working husband. Dad was surprised all right but he wasn't nearly as happy about the whole thing as she'd hoped. Still, the job got done and the horse survived with no lasting ill effects. Mom wasn't likely to let one little failure discourage her love of surprises for long. A good surprise was always one of her chief delights. Next time she'd just have to be better prepared.

Eyes Wide Open

EL Bevy Chevy

I bought my first car in Houston, Texas in 1978. It was a 1974 Chevy Malibu full size station wagon…very sexy. My roommate and I were two Canadian nurses working in Galveston at the time and we went halves on the car, hence the name EL Bevy Chevy. The EL stood for our last names, Edwards and Landry, and the Bevy Chevy was just because we liked the sound of it. My Dad, who was visiting at the time, gave us a little help in picking it out. Actually we had pictured buying one of those VW vans so we could travel in it but we were willing to settle for the station wagon. In a pinch you could sleep in the back and it did look easier to drive.

We got it home and Dad was careful to make sure we had the trunk loaded with emergency gear like booster cables, cans of oil and a funnel, electrical tape, and a few basic tools. Before he and Mom left to return to Canada, he also gave us quick instructions on how to check the various fluid levels, boost the battery and change a tire. It all looked simple enough. I can't tell you how exciting it was to have the kind of independence and freedom that owning that car gave us.

Of course it had its little quirks. A couple of months after we took ownership it started to belch blue smoke out the tailpipe. We thought we might be on fire but the mechanic said the rings were worn so that oil was leaking out. Replacing the rings would cost a fair chunk of change and we didn't have that kind of money. Instead we opted to

Eyes Wide Open

ignore the blue smoke and just keep adding oil every time we filled the gas tank. I confess we weren't thinking much about the environment at the time.

At the end of the year our work visas ran out and we decided to load everything up and drive back to Canada. It would be the longest road trip we'd ever attempted. We packed all our worldly goods into the back of the car, armed ourselves with a good map and set out heading north.

We hadn't even driven a full day when poor old EL Bevy Chevy just seemed to run out of steam and die. We coasted to a stop at the side of the road and I got out for a look under the hood. Perhaps it would be something really obvious. In point of fact the engine was covered in frothy pink foam and I couldn't even begin to imagine what that was all about. It looked like prayer was our best option. We weren't there long before a Good Samaritan came along and we learned the value of the items my Dad had stocked us with. It turned out that we'd blown a hole in a hose and the pink foam was our transmission fluid. The electrical tape temporarily fixed the hole and the can of oil would do as a substitute that would at least get us to the next town and a garage where we could get everything properly repaired.

You'd think that was enough excitement for one trip but two days later we came out of the motel we'd stayed in to find one of the tires completely flat. No problem this time. We pulled out the jack and the spare tire and went to work. We wouldn't win any prizes for speed but between the two of us we managed to jack the car up, remove the flat

Eyes Wide Open

tire and get the spare put on. We were feeling very competent as we tightened the last of the little nut thingy's and stood back to admire our handiwork. Oh foolish pride! Imagine our humiliation when we realized neither one of us had any idea of how to lower the jack and we were going to have to ask for help after all. The gentleman who came to our assistance was having difficulty keeping a straight face as he flipped the little lever on the jack to enable him to crank it down again.

We did make it back to Canada safely and I bought out the other half of the car so EL Bevy Chevy became my own as my roommate and I went our separate ways. By then I'd become quite attached to the old girl. We had history together. In the end she played a big part in the early days of my relationship with Bev, the man I would eventually marry. He had a pickup truck and whenever my car broke down or refused to start in some parking lot, he would come to my rescue and use his truck to tow us to the nearest garage. He was my hero and EL Bevy Chevy gave him lots of opportunities to shine. I loved that car.

Eyes Wide Open

Hercules

When I was a child we loved catching insects of all sorts. An empty glass jar and a hammer and nail to punch some air holes in the lid were all we needed and the hunt would be on. No grasshopper or cricket was safe from pursuit. Bumble bees were the trickiest because they tended to fight back. I'll never forget the day I turned over a log at school and discovered the biggest spider I'd ever seen in my life. It was gray and looked positively muscular with thick hairy legs like a tarantula. When I brought it home in my jar Dad said it was a wood spider. I named him Hercules.

We were living in a little mining subdivision nestled in the woods south of the highway between Blind River and Spragge with Georgian Bay on one side and the railway tracks next to the highway on the other. There were about two dozen houses and not much else so we children made our own fun. We had the run of the woods and did a lot of exploring and building forts. Whenever two children got into a tiff everyone would choose sides and the mock war would be on. It was a favorite game that somehow never got out of hand. We would send out spies, take prisoners, and do our best to destroy one another's forts until one side or the other gave up.

The battle I remember best was the one Hercules played a part in. We were having a strategy meeting in a tent in our back yard when it suddenly occurred to me that we had a readymade secret weapon in Hercules. I dashed into the house and brought out the big pickle jar that housed

Eyes Wide Open

my captured spider. My fellow warriors were duly impressed and we resolved to make him part of our arsenal. Excitement ran high as we marched out to the road to confront our opponents. They were there all right, waiting for us to emerge. Someone yelled "Charge", and we all ran straight at them shouting "Hercules…Hercules!"

My job was to run out in front with the pickle jar held in my outstretched hands as both shield and sword. It worked! They fled like rabbits with a pack of dogs after them. The war was over and we were victorious.

Looking back, I doubt they even knew what was in the jar. Our excess of confidence was probably what unnerved them. Nevertheless, Hercules was the hero of the hour. We retired to our tent and prepared to reward him. I don't know who came up with the idea but it was decided that each one of us would pay our respects by reaching a hand into the jar to touch him. He was part of the team after all. It was all very exciting not to mention seriously creepy.

I kept Hercules for a few more days before deciding that he deserved better than life in a pickle jar. I took him out to the woods and found a spot where a tree had fallen and was starting to rot. It looked like a place that would appeal to a wood spider so I opened the jar and tipped him out. In seconds he was gone but I've never forgotten him. He was certainly the most impressive creature I ever caught in one of my jars.

Eyes Wide Open

Bathing Suit Blues

There isn't a woman on earth who hasn't struggled at some time in her life with the question of body image. I was a "late bloomer". In fact, by the time Grade 7 rolled around and I still showed no signs of the curves the other girls were sporting, I began to wonder if I would ever bloom at all. At least I wasn't the only one. Sally and I became friends out of our shared flat-chested misery. None of the boys were making fools of themselves over us. I overheard someone tell the boy I'd had a crush on all year that I liked him. It was one of those times I wished I'd listened when my mother warned me of the perils of eavesdropping. His response was "Her? She's got nothing!" Obviously, breasts were the only thing that counted.

Sally and I spent a lot of time trying to figure out a way to speed up whatever development was destined to happen. I remember one discussion behind the closed doors of my room where she insisted that she'd heard that placing ice cubes on your breasts for as long as you could stand it would do the trick. It didn't seem logical so we just laughed at the idea. A couple of days later we both confessed that we had secretly tried it. After all, what did we really know?

That summer we tried stuffing socks into our shirts just to see what we would look like with a figure. After much careful adjusting and a few safety pins to safeguard against disasters like slippage, we even ventured outside for

Eyes Wide Open

a walk down the road. Of course we made sure no one we knew was likely to see us.

How well I remember the bathing suit my mother bought me that year. A bathing suit was something I couldn't inherit from my older brothers and my mom didn't think she could sew one so I was going to get something brand new from the store. We didn't have a lot of money so she decided she would get it a size or two bigger than I really needed at the time. That way I could grow into it and it would last more than a year. She bought a two piece suit that had an actual bra with fairly stiff cups that could stand on their own even without breasts to fill them.

We went camping a lot and I loved walking around campgrounds where nobody knew me wearing that bathing suit. I felt like a million bucks. Unfortunately, getting it wet could sometimes result in extremely embarrassing cave-ins. I couldn't possibly go swimming when there was always the danger that I would stand up only to discover that one of my so-called breasts was accidentally inverted and pointing in the wrong direction.

We moved when I was in Grade 8 and I never saw Sally again. I assume she must have finally blossomed in the end. In spite of all our fears it was inevitable after all. By the time I got to High School I was finally wearing a 32AA bra and had had my first period. That old bathing suit was still too big and eventually I replaced it. I never did have a figure that would catch anybody's attention and to top it off I turned out to be smart. No boys would be chasing me any time soon. Somehow in the midst of it all I

Eyes Wide Open

realized that that didn't really bother me. I had good friends both male and female among the group of students the rest of the school called 'Browners', short for 'Brown-nosers' because we got good grades. I found I actually liked myself.

Getting my period hadn't turned out to be such a picnic after all so I reasoned that having a boyfriend was probably just as likely to result in all kinds of unforeseen pitfalls. Being a woman was going to be about a lot more than breasts and what the boys thought of my figure. What was I in such a big hurry for anyway?

Eyes Wide Open

Brothers

When our boys were three and four years old we lived in a small two bedroom house on a farm just north of Arthur, Ontario. With our daughter approaching her first birthday things were a little crowded. All three children were sharing a small bedroom with the crib and a set of bunk beds crowded in together.

Daniel, being the oldest, had been relegated to the top bunk. He had already discovered the hard way that a certain degree of caution was needed when playing or sleeping in his lofty nest. Fortunately for him, his one fall had landed him neatly in the open drawer of the dresser standing next to the bed. Apart from a couple of bruises on the backs of his legs he survived his accident with no lasting harm done.

One day when I was working in another part of the house, Jason, always and forever a climber, decided to join his brother up top. I had no idea he was up there until I heard a scuffle followed by Daniel's heart wrenching drawn out cry of "He-e-e-l-l-p!!" Panic lent wings to my feet and I made it to the bedroom in record time. There was my three year old Jason hanging upside down from the top bunk with his brother stretched out above him grasping his ankles in a desperate attempt to stop his fall. He couldn't have held him much longer. In fact, I don't know how he was holding him at all. They were almost the same size after all but Daniel's face wore a grimace of stubborn determination that I have since come to know well. He just refused to let go.

Eyes Wide Open

His relief was palpable when I came to the rescue and took the weight from his straining arms.

Jason learned caution on the bunk bed that day but it wasn't the last time he got himself into a fix with his climbing. Daniel was always the one to go for help whenever his brother got stuck in some impossible situation. We would be sitting peacefully in a campsite somewhere and Daniel would come running. "Dad, you better bring a rope. Jason is on a ledge halfway up a cliff and he can't get up or down." Or I would be making supper and Daniel would burst through the door with a shout of "Mom, Jason's stuck on the roof." Of course, that's another story.

Eventually they grew up. None of Jason's experiences spoiled his love of climbing. He spent five years as a roofer when he was paying for college and now he climbs for sport. Daniel hasn't had to come to his rescue in years but back when they were boys he was definitely his brother's keeper. That's the great thing about brothers. They're there when you need them.

Eyes Wide Open

Grab That Bird

     Hunting was a part of life when I was growing up. My Dad enjoyed it immensely but he never did it just for sport. It put meat on the table and that was important. I've seen those jokes where "you know you're Canadian when every fall your kitchen turns into a butcher shop". Well, that was true at our house. The meat, whether it was venison or moose, or even bear, would get cut and wrapped in butcher paper and stored safely in the big chest freezer. Smaller game like rabbit or partridge usually got eaten the same day it was killed.

     My younger brother Tom and I often went along when Dad was hunting small game. We'd follow behind him as he stalked through the woods, doing our level best to walk without stepping on twigs or otherwise making unnecessary noise as we navigated through the tangled brush. I loved to pretend we were frontiersmen and that our survival depended on our success in the hunt. Our heads would turn from side to side as we searched the trees around us, hoping to spot something before Dad did. We never could though. It was like he had x-ray vision or something. He'd stop suddenly and swing the gun up. That was our cue to freeze and we'd hold our breath wondering what on earth he was looking at. He was an excellent shot so we rarely had to go home empty handed.

     Our job was to carry the game so on one occasion when Dad shot a partridge he sent Tom off to collect it. Tom went bounding off in the direction Dad had pointed,

Eyes Wide Open

scanning the ground as he went. The bird was there all right and without hesitation he reached out to take hold of it. He jumped back in startled dismay when the bird at his feet suddenly burst into the air with a mad flapping of outstretched wings. It only went a short distance before settling back to earth so Tom reasoned that it must be wounded and its short flight was merely the last gasp before death overtook it.

He began his approach with more caution the second time. The partridge lay perfectly still…surely it wasn't breathing. He heaved a sigh of relief and bent to retrieve it. His involuntary shout echoed in the stillness and he jerked his hand back as the partridge seemed to come to life. Once again it took to the air only to land twenty feet away. By then Tom was beginning to get annoyed so he rushed to the spot where the uncooperative bird had touched down only to have it flutter off and settle beyond his reach one more time.

He looked up at the sound of Dad's voice calling his name. When he turned to look back the way he'd come he spotted Dad, a broad smile on his face, holding up the partridge he had shot and beckoning him to return. He glanced back at the bird he'd been chasing. The fool thing wasn't wounded at all and was probably laughing at him.

Eyes Wide Open

Horrible Haircuts

Have you ever found yourself seated on a kitchen chair draped in one of your mother's tablecloths while one or the other of your parents circled you with a pair of scissors and a frown of concentration on their faces? That's what getting a haircut meant in our house. My Dad would trim away, stand back for a critical examination and reach out to trim some more. My hair had some curl in it so getting the bangs straight was challenging. Just when he thought he'd managed it he would spot a few strands longer than the rest and take another snip. That's how I often ended up with ragged inch long stubble sticking out in every direction instead of the bangs I was hoping for.

You would think I might have learned something from my childhood experiences and opted to let the professionals handle haircuts for my own children but I was convinced I could do better than my Dad. Consequently, all three of my children have had their chance to sit on that kitchen chair. For the most part I did do better. I bought a set of electric clippers that came with a video and several attachments that insured a uniform cut at the length of your choice. What could be simpler? My daughter's hair would still have to be cut with scissors but the men of the house could all get clipped. It would be virtually impossible to mess up, or so I thought.

There came a Saturday when the boys were beginning to look quite shaggy so "Mom's Barber Shop" was declared open. By then I had already accomplished

Eyes Wide Open

several successful haircuts using the new clippers and I was feeling quite confident. Jason, who was in Grade 7 at the time, was perched on the chair with his feet drawn up under the tablecloth I had pinned around his neck. His younger sister, Lauren, was watching the proceedings with considerable interest. Jason flinched when the clippers caught his hair and complained that it was pulling. I assured him that I could easily fix the problem.

A bit of oil was probably all that was needed so I removed the attachment and carefully dribbled a few drops onto the exposed blades. I let it run for a moment to make sure everything was well lubricated before proceeding with the haircut from the spot where I'd left off, taking one long swipe up the back of Jason's bowed head.

I realized too late that I had forgotten to replace the attachment on the clippers. I turned them off and gazed in horrified fascination at the long naked stripe running up the back of my son's dark head. Lauren sucked in her breath and clapped a hand over her mouth. Jason wasn't sure what the problem was but he could see his sister's face and that was enough for him. He jumped up and headed to the nearest mirror with me only steps behind him. One look and he took off for his bedroom where he could hide his misery behind a closed door. He swore he was never coming out. We both cried as I begged his forgiveness and tried to come up with some solution. A hat couldn't begin to cover it.

It was my husband, Bev, who finally saved the day. Jason had a set of pastels in his art box and Bev found one

Eyes Wide Open

that was the exact shade of brown to match his hair. He simply colored in the exposed scalp thereby effectively disguising it. He then proposed to Jason that we attend church as usual the next day to find out if anyone noticed anything strange about his haircut.

Jason was a bit nervous but his confidence grew as it became obvious that no one could tell there was a problem. That settled it. Every morning for the two weeks it took for his own hair to fill in the gap Bev would use the crayon to touch up the color on the back of Jason's head disguising the stripe that my mistake had put there. No one at school ever noticed a thing. He did forgive me but he never let me cut his hair again. Neither did Bev. The clippers were relegated to a back corner of the bathroom cupboard where they have been gathering dust for years.

I did get to cut my Dad's hair a time or two during my brief career as a home hairstylist. It was an odd feeling to have our roles reversed. They say that what goes around comes around but I hope that doesn't always hold true. I hate to imagine myself seated in the dreaded chair one day at the mercy of Jason and a pair of scissors.

Eyes Wide Open

Intrepid Voyageurs

Bev and I went on a canoe trip - for extreme trekkers it might not have actually qualified as a real canoe trip. There were no arduous portages and our camp, once set up, stayed set up until we were ready to come home. Instead of the sleek lightweight canoes that most trekkers favor, we used a Sportspal. It certainly is lightweight but it doesn't glide easily through the water at every stroke of the paddle. It's designed more for duck hunting than canoe trekking. Some liken it to trying to paddle a bathtub across a lake but we weren't in a hurry so we didn't mind. We like it because it is nice and wide and consequently very stable. That will count more and more as we get older and our balance becomes an issue. Besides, it brings back a lot of memories.

The first canoe my younger brother, Tom, bought with his own money was a Sportspal. He spent many happy hours on the water in that boat. We were nearly done High School when my two older brothers conceived a plan for the greatest wilderness adventure of their lives.

They would take the whole summer and canoe all the way to James Bay and they would borrow Tom's Sportspal to do it in. They bought huge backpacks from the army surplus store. Dave learned how to make Indian bannock and began to plan for the food staples they would need to carry. They were counting on supplementing their diet by fishing and hunting along the way so Richard bought a crossbow. There were no cell phones back then

Eyes Wide Open

but they did think to carry whistles in case they got separated.

The day came when everything was ready and we drove them north to their chosen put in spot near Chapleau. The canoe was loaded to maximum capacity and excitement ran high as we said our farewells. No explorer ever set out with greater anticipation and hope of adventure than those two. They had no idea just how short their trek was destined to be.

They hadn't gone more than six kilometers when they came to a set of rapids. With the canoe as heavily laden as it was they decided to portage the packs. Richard would walk along the shore and guide the canoe down the rapids by means of a rope. It was a method called "lining the canoe" that neither of them had ever actually tried before. Meanwhile, Dave would begin the task of carrying the packs to a point beyond the rapids.

The big square 80 pound packs were cumbersome and Dave was struggling to adjust to the weight when he tripped and fell on what turned out to be a wasp nest. Angry wasps swarmed upward to surround him and he instantly forgot the weight on his back as he scrambled up and took off running through the bush. He soon left the wasps behind and finally came to a gasping halt on the bank of the river once more. He just managed to ease the pack from his aching shoulders when he heard the desperate tweeting of Richard's emergency whistle coming from around a bend in the river.

Eyes Wide Open

Before Dave could respond Richard himself appeared at the bend looking like thunder. He was drenched from head to toe and there was no sign of the canoe. Apparently "lining the canoe" down the rapids wasn't as easy as it sounded. At a particularly rough patch the lightweight aluminum Sportspal had spun out of control on the end of the rope turning sideways so that it was caught by a huge wave. Richard, who still held the rope, ended up losing his precarious balance and got pulled into the river. He had to let go in order to save himself but the canoe wasn't going anywhere. It was folded almost in half around a boulder and the rushing water kept it pinned there..

It took their combined strength to eventually pry it loose. Even though they managed to stomp it back into shape it didn't much resemble the canoe they had started out with. The ribs were broken and it was holed pretty badly. It was 'fix it' or 'walk' so they opted to attempt repairs. They spent two days making new ribs for it from some nearby cedar and sealing the holes with the patch kit they'd brought along.

When they put it back in the water it actually floated but it was obvious the patches weren't going to hold very well. It was leaking badly when they set out once more. Progress was slow as they had to spend as much time bailing as paddling. They made it as far as the next lake and decided that was as far as either of them was willing to go. Fortunately there was a fishing lodge on the lake and the people there offered a means to return to civilization. They were happy to take a break from their exertions and camped there for a week or so before heading home.

Eyes Wide Open

The great adventure was at an end less than 20 kilometers from where it began. Strangely enough, they didn't seem at all disappointed. They came away with at least one good story and it only cost them the price of Tom's canoe…oh, and one crossbow which is probably still somewhere at the bottom of the river.

Eyes Wide Open

The Things We Do For Love

The very first Christmas Bev and I spent together was one to remember. We were officially a couple and I was in love. What sort of gift do you give in that situation? Nothing I could think of seemed appropriate. I wanted a gift that would be a symbol of the depth of my feelings. The sorts of things I could afford didn't have the significance that I was looking for. In the end I decided I would make something and it would be a labor of love. I liked the sound of that. The only problem was I was a little short on the requisite skills. Let's just say that handwork was not my strong suit.

Fortunately my friend, Nora Lea, was more than willing to coach me along. I decided I would attempt to knit something. I had learned to knit and purl as a child but never did keep it up. The project would have to be something impressive that didn't require anything other than those two basic stitches. I had my eye on these wonderful hand knit pullover ski sweaters that Nora assured me were easy to create. The whole thing was done on a round needle, which actually looks more like two needles joined together by a long flexible plastic cord. It was just about as basic as you could get.

The sweater in the pattern I chose had a band of huge snowflakes across the chest but she insisted that anyone who could count stitches would have no problem with it. I bought the needle, the pattern, and wool in the

Eyes Wide Open

same blue as Bev's eyes along with a couple of skeins of white for the snowflakes and I was in business.

Some people say they find knitting to be relaxing but I'm sure they must be lying. That's probably because I never did manage to achieve the easy competency with the needles that expert knitters have. I know my mother could watch television while she worked and sweaters would magically grow under her flying fingers and busily clacking needles.

As for me, it seemed the needles possessed a life of their own and if I did not grip them tightly and focus with fierce concentration on what I was doing they simply refused to submit to my control. One moment's inattention would result in botched work that would have to be ripped out and redone.

From time to time I was convinced the instructions were written in Chinese and I would have to call Nora Lea to serve as an interpreter. It was proving to be tougher than I expected but I was far too stubborn to quit once I'd started. Progress was slow so I began to carry it with me to work. I was on the night shift at the hospital and if it was a quiet night I could spend hours on my project. I would work at it doggedly until my hands cramped up and I couldn't straighten my fingers.

Gradually, the results of my efforts grew to look like a sweater and when the snowflakes emerged actually looking like snowflakes I was thrilled. I was nearly done working on the sleeves when I began to have an uneasy

Eyes Wide Open

sense that something was wrong. I'd followed the directions exactly but the sleeves looked as though they would end up at least four inches short. After countless hours of blood, sweat and tears the whole thing was going to be ruined and I was frantic.

One quick call brought Nora Lea rushing to my assistance one more time. She took one look and told me that the sleeves ended up short because my knitting was much tighter than what the pattern called for. She saved the day by knitting a couple of cuffs and crocheting them onto the ends of the sleeves. By the time she was done it looked as though they were meant to be there.

The sweater was beautiful but it felt a little stiff and heavy. In point of fact, the whole thing was knitted so tightly that it could stand up all by itself like a suit of armor. I tried washing it with a lot of fabric softener but it didn't make much difference. In the end I wrapped it up and gave it to Bev along with a note in which I'd calculated the exact number of stitches that had gone into it, every one of which was a painful expression of my love for him.

He was duly impressed and actually attempted to wear it once. Unfortunately, the "suit of armor" description was almost literal. It seemed that even air couldn't penetrate those tightly knit stitches. He very nearly cooked in it. It may not have stopped bullets but it certainly would have slowed them down. He stoutly assured me that it would be perfect in case he ever went on an expedition to the Arctic and in light of that he kept it for years. Each time

Eyes Wide Open

we moved he would lovingly pack it in along with the rest of the clothes.

It was my one and only knitting project. I've never been tempted to try another. As a Christmas gift that spoke of love it was a huge success. As a sweater….well, not so much.

Eyes Wide Open

Changrak and Su-Ling

I have a fondness for cats. When my brother, Tom, and I were children we visited a farm where we were offered one of the barn cats as a pet. We wanted one in the worst way and so we begged Mom and Dad to allow us to say yes. Mom wasn't keen on the idea at first. It took us a couple of weeks to wear her down. Eventually she consented to give it a try but she was adamant that she did not want a scruffy barn cat in the house. She decided to search the newspapers and the little notices pinned on the board at the Laundromat for something more appropriate.

The net result was that we became the proud owners of not one cat but two. Apparently they came as a set. No kittens for us…Changrak and Su-Ling were two full grown Siamese cats. They had always been together and their previous owner wouldn't hear of separating them.

Changrak, the male, was a handsome Seal Point and looked like I thought all Siamese cats looked…almost white with a brown face, tail, and legs. Su-Ling, however, was a Chocolate Point. She was brown with a black face, tail, and legs. She was the smaller of the two and quite timid. It took a little work to win her trust but with Changrak setting the example she soon came around.

I've heard some people say that Siamese cats are temperamental and not very friendly but we never saw any of that with our two. It wasn't long before they became an integral part of the family. They were good company and always entertaining to watch. When they hunted they looked like miniature panthers stalking their prey. They would creep along with infinite caution, their bodies low to the ground, the tips of their outstretched tails twitching furiously just before they pounced. I could easily imagine them in the jungle somewhere. It was like having National Geographic come to life before our eyes.

Once summer came and they were allowed outside it wouldn't be unusual to hear Changrak at the door, his loud and insistent meows summoning us to see whatever small creature he'd caught. He always brought them home and we would try to show him that we were duly impressed....except for the time he released a live mouse in the middle of the living room in front of my parents' guests. That got everyone hopping.

I'm not sure there is another animal on earth that can relax the way a cat can. Changrak loved to sprawl on his back, completely limp with legs pointing in four different directions and what looked like a contented smile on his inscrutable face. If Su-Ling happened to be curled up on someone's lap that would be the exact spot Changrak wanted for his own nap. Nothing else would do.

He would sidle up next to her and begin his campaign to appropriate her warm nest by licking her face and rubbing foreheads with her in seeming affection. She never failed to respond by relaxing under his tender ministrations. In moments she would be completely lulled, relaxed to the point of bonelessness. Then, in her moment of greatest vulnerability, Changrak would give her a mighty sideways heave, knocking her completely off her perch to land in an undignified heap on the floor. Without a second glance he would settle himself comfortably in her vacated spot purring in unashamed contentment.

He used that same strategy time after time and she never seemed to learn from past experience. He was obviously the brains of the outfit....or maybe she just figured the attention was worth it.

Eyes Wide Open

Goodnight John-Boy

My Mom had a hilarious sense of fun and adventure. The first 13 years of her life were not happy ones and so in a sense, she missed her own childhood. Once she had her own family she was determined to experience the all the fun she'd missed. No one loved a good joke or a surprise more than she did. You never knew when you'd find a rubber spider in your cup and games of any sort would inevitably end up being very lively indeed if she was participating. There was a lot of laughter in our house as I was growing up. The Bible says a cheerful heart is good medicine and I know that to be true.

One of my many favorite memories is of a visit home by my oldest brother, Richard, when my younger brother and I were around 12 and 13. Richard was 10 years older than me and we hadn't seen him in quite some time. We lived in an old farmhouse with a huge open area upstairs. The boys had beds out in the open area and there were two small rooms partitioned off with paper thin walls for my parents and me. Bedtime often involved conversations through the walls followed by a round of "goodnights" between all of us. Someone would always throw out a "goodnight John-Boy" at the end. We were fans of the Waltons at the time.

On this particular occasion as we all lay there in the dark, my mother was making observations about how thin Richard looked to her and asking him if he was getting enough to eat.

Richard groaned and fired back with an exasperated "Ma, I'm not thin…you should see my tits!"

Her instant response was "Richard, in this house we do not say tits". There was a moment of embarrassed silence before she added in serious and extremely righteous tones, "In this house we say titties".

The entire family erupted in peals of unrestrained laughter, the kind that has you falling off the bed or wondering if you're about to pee your pants. Just when things would begin to calm down someone would snicker and we'd be off again. It was quite a while before we could control our giggles enough to say goodnight to the fictional "John-Boy".

Eyes Wide Open

Don't Pet the Wildlife

We've had our share of wildlife sightings on our summer travels. The most recent was of a black bear we passed on one of our hikes in Northern Ontario. The bear was a good distance off the trail but the undergrowth was sparse and we were able to watch him for several minutes as he made his way through the scattered hardwoods. It was a rare treat, one my Dad would have appreciated. He never missed an opportunity to study the animals he encountered in the woods. Occasionally, he got to study them much closer than common sense might have allowed.

He was returning from a fishing trip somewhere around the time I was born when he noticed what appeared to be a large animal swimming across the lake in the distance ahead of him. Curious, he angled the boat for a closer look. As he approached he realized that it was a bear...a female with three small cubs swimming along behind her. Had they been on land he would have given them a very wide berth indeed. A mother bear with cubs is not to be trifled with. As it was, he could bring the boat right alongside with total impunity. She was helpless to do anything about it without solid ground under her feet.

Afterwards he could not really explain what he did next. He acted on impulse. Certainly, he didn't think it through very well. In any case, he eased the boat up next to the last cub in the line and reached out to grab it by the scruff of the neck. With one heave he plucked it right out of the lake and into the boat at his feet before speeding away.

Eyes Wide Open

Perhaps he imagined raising the cub himself. What better way to learn about bears? By the time he reached the shore at the far end of the lake he knew he'd have to fashion a leash of some kind or risk getting badly scratched. He was beginning to have second thoughts about the whole thing but it was too late to undo it all by then.

It caused quite an uproar when he came home from his fishing trip leading a bear cub on a rope. In the end they had to lock the poor thing in the garden shed as there was no other safe place to put it. No one slept that night. Who could have imagined the terrible racket that one small cub could make in an enclosed space? The noise had everyone on edge. By morning Dad was feeling pretty bad about the whole thing and thoroughly regretting his impulsive decision.

The cub only spent that one night in the shed. There was a man who ran a gas station out at the highway. He kept animals in his own makeshift zoo for the tourists to look at and he agreed to take the little bear and raise it. Dad would stop there from time to time to check in on the bear he pulled out of the water but I think if he had the chance to do it all over again he would have left that mother bear and her cubs to cross the lake in peace.

Eyes Wide Open

Pass the Groundhog

When our children were young we had the privilege of meeting and getting to know a wonderful young couple from Nigeria. David was here working towards completing his PhD and he and his wife, Eno, became very much a part of our family for the years they were in Canada.

David, an avid sportsman, developed an interest in archery very early on in his stay. Living in an apartment made practicing difficult so visits to the farm became perfect opportunities to hone his skills. Of course, the boys were fascinated and never tired of watching, their fingers twitching in their eagerness to try it for themselves.

They got their wish when David presented them with their own bows on Christmas Day. He had fashioned them from the materials at hand….good, pliable branches stripped of their bark and smoothed to a fine sheen, notched and strung with heavy twine. They could hardly wait to bundle up and head outside to test them.

David's enthusiasm was hard to resist. Later that summer when we were all visiting Grandma and Grandpa Livingston's farm in Markdale, he decided to go hunting with his bow. All three children clamored to go with him. I'll never forget the sight of them out in the field the grain had come off of. David was on his hands and knees making a very careful approach to a groundhog they'd spotted sitting in the sun. It wouldn't be easy to get close enough for a shot without the groundhog noticing him and scooting

Eyes Wide Open

back into its hole. The rest of us watched as he patiently stalked his prey with three small children on their hands and knees strung out in single file behind him like ducklings of decreasing size, each one intent on mimicking his every move.

David got his groundhog in the end and he was eager to try cooking it over a slow fire in the yard once we got home. Hours later it was well and truly smoked but we had to finish it in the oven so it would be ready in time to include with the rest of our dinner. We had a couple of extra boys at the table that night but there was enough for everyone to have a taste. One of our young visitors announced with great dignity that he didn't eat small rodents. The other was frankly horrified so we quickly assured them both that there were plenty of other choices and no one expected them to eat the groundhog. The rest of us were made of more adventurous stuff and we each took a portion. The first bite might have been tentative but it wasn't long before we were all grinning at one another. It tasted like ham.

David and Eno had an impact on all our lives. Their endless patience, love, and Godly example as well as their willingness and even eagerness to try new things made them role models to our children that we treasured. They will never be forgotten. Our lives were richer and certainly more interesting for having shared those times with them.

Many years later our daughter, Lauren, was doing an ice-breaker activity in her Grade 12 environmental science class. Each student had to list four things they had done

Eyes Wide Open

with only three of the four being true. Everyone else would then try to guess which of the things listed was false. Lauren's list raised a few eyebrows. It included shooting a porcupine, riding an elephant, driving a dogsled, and eating a groundhog. Apparently that was a hard one to beat.

Eyes Wide Open

Blame It on the Smoke Detector

The upstairs apartment I lived in when Bev and I were dating was in an older four-plex across the street from a Public School in Sudbury. It was a quiet building with my landlord living just below me. My apartment was cozy and bright with plenty of space. There was even a door from the kitchen opening onto a tiny railed balcony that sat on the roof of my landlord's porch. I eventually got used to the orange plaid carpet in the living room. It didn't clash too badly with my furniture if I covered the couch with a blanket. Fortunately, the flowers on my second hand swivel rocker were also orange. Okay, perhaps it was a decorator's nightmare but I wasn't hard to please in those days. At least it had character. All in all, it was the best I'd had since moving back to the city the previous year. The appliances were in decent shape and there'd even been a brand new smoke detector recently installed in the kitchen.

I decided to invest in a little hibachi that I could place out on my balcony so I could barbecue and I invited Bev to come over for dinner so we could try it out. We got the charcoal lit and as soon as the briquettes were burning hot enough we tossed on our hamburgers. Bev squatted by the barbecue and took over the burger flipping and I crowded out onto the balcony to keep him company and admire his flipping technique. It was going well till I noticed that the smoke was blowing right into the kitchen through the screen door. I had an instant vision of that brand new smoke detector and imagined my landlord's reaction if it suddenly blasted out it's shrill warning that

Eyes Wide Open

something I was attempting to cook was about to burst into flames. I felt embarrassed just thinking about it so I reached in and pulled the inner door shut to keep the smoke out.

It locked. I stood with my hand on the doorknob, my face burning with mortification - so much for making a good impression. I felt like an absolute idiot. When Bev asked what was wrong I had to swallow a couple of times before I could get the words out.

"I've locked us out," I admitted in a very small voice. He stood up to try the knob himself.

"Yup, it's locked all right," he conceded before calmly returning to his former position squatting by the hibachi. "First things first though. These hamburgers are almost done."

How could he be so calm? We were probably going to have to shout for help till someone got the landlord to come up and let us in. I was never going to live this down. I fretted and stewed for five more minutes till Bev handed me the plate of burgers and leaned out to look over the railing.

"I think I can climb down," he announced.

I started to protest that he didn't even have shoes on but he was already over the rail and lowering himself to hang from his arms and jump to the top step of the porch below him. I fervently hoped my landlord wasn't looking

Eyes Wide Open

out the window at that very moment. I couldn't imagine what he would think to see a man's jean clad legs and stocking feet dangling in the air outside his kitchen. It was probably a vain hope because when Bev knocked on his door a moment later and stood there in his socks asking him if he'd mind opening the door to my apartment, he never batted an eye. He just smiled and fetched the key with no questions asked. I suppose he had a window open and heard the whole thing. I'm sure it was more entertaining than the evening news. It took me at least until dessert to see the humour in the whole thing. We ended up having a good chuckle and wishing we'd had a camera to capture the moment. Even so, I could hardly look my landlord in the eye the next time I went to pay my rent.

We drove past the old place on our last visit to Sudbury. It's looking a bit run down after 30 years but the balcony still sits perched above the porch the same way it did back when we were dating. These days the railing is lopsided and aged to a silver grey with only a few tattered paint flecks to show that it was once a pristine white. I glanced fondly at the man sitting next to me in the car. I may not have made much of an impression that day but he married me anyway.

Eyes Wide Open

Not Quite Harmless

I was biking along the Georgian Trail this past weekend and twice nearly came to grief when I narrowly missed running over a garter snake slithering across the path almost directly under my wheels. There is something about the way a snake moves that is both beautiful and repulsive at the same time. Their speed can be unnerving though in both of these encounters it was probably what saved them. I clutched desperately at the brakes and went into a spastic sort of front wheel wobble as I skirted past the first one.

The second was even closer. I was convinced that a collision was inevitable and my shoulders hunched reflexively as I pictured what would happen. Something that small wasn't likely to survive the encounter. I don't much like snakes but that didn't mean I wanted to coast right over it like an unexpected speed bump. I was hugely relieved when it slipped past and disappeared in the tall grass edging the trail with only an inch or so to spare.

Garter snakes are harmless enough. I grew up believing that they didn't have teeth and so, of course, that's what I told my children when they mentioned seeing one in Grandma Livingston's garden. My daughter, Lauren, would have been around five years old at the time and she and her brother, Jason, who was seven, decided they would try to capture it. No doubt they had visions of producing it at the dinner table for maximum effect. It was bound to be worth a shriek or two.

Eyes Wide Open

They set out for the garden and began to hunt through the rows of vegetables for their unsuspecting prey. It looked like an enterprise that would keep them occupied for the afternoon so I left them to it and went to work in another part of the yard. When they finally discovered the garter snake sunning itself between the peas and carrots they discovered it wasn't going to be as easy to grab as they'd expected. It was fast, much faster than they were. There was a bit of a scramble and Jason got a foot on its tail effectively pinning it in place. The snake thrashed about frantically trying to free itself.

"Grab it around the neck," he urged, waving an arm at his younger sister. Without a second thought she reached out to do just that.

That's when we discovered that garter snakes do indeed have teeth. Lauren's startled shout caused Jason to jerk his foot back and the snake took advantage of the moment to beat a hasty retreat. I looked over to see the two of them with their heads together examining Lauren's hand. She finally came running to me, sporting two tiny puncture marks on the end of her finger. It actually drew blood.

"You said they didn't bite," Jason accused. Lauren looked ready to cry.

"Well," I hedged. "If someone stepped on your foot so you couldn't get away and then tried to grab you around the neck, you'd bite them too. You scared that poor snake half to death and he was pretty desperate to get away."

Eyes Wide Open

That was a point they were willing to concede. You have to respect an animal's instinct to fight back when it's trapped. There was no further snake hunting that afternoon. In fact, the garter snakes of the world have had nothing to fear from the Livingston's since that day…unless of course they are trying to cross a bike path in front of one of us.

Eyes Wide Open

A Force to be Reckoned With

My parents moved to Guelph when my Dad was in his early seventies. He was never entirely comfortable living in the city. I think he expected to get mugged every time he went for a walk in the park. He made himself a good solid cane that he began carrying long before he had any need of one. If anyone had ever actually tried to mug him they would have gotten much more than they'd bargained for. He fully intended to use that cane to defend himself. Fortunately, Guelph is a fairly safe city and he never had occasion to prove he wasn't a helpless old man by knocking some hapless would be attacker over the head.

My Dad was tall and lean and much stronger than most people would guess by looking at him. As a young man he had quite a reputation among the miners he worked with. He'd been seen to bend spikes with his bare hands. Once, when his Model-A Ford had a flat and there was no jack he simply lifted the corner of the vehicle and held it until his brother could roll a stone into position to prop it up high enough for them to change the tire.

My brother, Richard, remembers Dad challenging him and three of his teen-aged friends to try to lift one end of an 800 pound rail. They tried mightily and weren't able to budge it an inch even with all four of them lifting together. Dad just smiled at their efforts before taking the end of the rail in his two hands and heaving it up to waist height. For good measure he then squatted, shifted his grip

Eyes Wide Open

and slowly raised it above his head. The boys just stood there gaping in awe.

Dad wasn't ever one to start a fight but heaven help whoever was foolish enough to throw a punch in his direction. He didn't back down when it came to protecting himself or the people he cared about. That was the case the day there was a Miner's Union picnic held at our house some time before I was born.

They had a pig and a lamb roasting on spits out in the yard and zinc washtubs filled with ice and beer. All the food was set up outside. The house had no indoor bathroom…just the outhouse at the back, so no one would have any reason to go inside. That was exactly the way my parents wanted it. They had just bought a new couch and chair and my mother was concerned about something getting spilled on it. New furniture was a rare luxury.

Things got a little rowdy as the afternoon faded into early evening. Everyone had just eaten and someone who'd had a little too much beer wandered into the house looking for a bathroom that wasn't there. A number of people simply followed him in, completely forgetting my Dad's request that the party stay outside. He knew my mother wouldn't be happy about it so he hurried in and began trying to usher everyone out again.

An argument started between two miners and it escalated as tempers flared. They were both big men and Dad stepped between them just as one of them took a swing at the other.

Eyes Wide Open

The blow landed square on my Dad's jaw and rocked him back on his heels. He believed it was deliberately aimed at him and he flew into a rage at being attacked in his own home. That miner never knew what hit him. Dad simply picked him up by the neck and pinned him to the wall as though he weighed nothing. When two others tried to grab his arms and pull him away he threw them both off. A fourth man joined the fray, catching him in a crushing bear hug, lifting him off his feet and attempting to squeeze the breath out of him. He just couldn't hold onto him. Dad broke free and in the resulting mayhem, the stove pipe got knocked off and a cloud of black soot billowed out to settle on everything including the new couch and chair. It was like being doused with cold water.

The fight was over but so was the party. It was obvious that my Dad was still angry and no one wanted to chance having that anger turned on them. A few friends stayed to help clean up the mess but most people made their apologies and headed for home.

I doubt it was the first fight my Dad ever got into but, as far as I know, it was the last. Word got around and the other miners treated him with a wary respect. They'd learned the hard way that he was a match for any four of them.

Eyes Wide Open

Tarzan of the Poplars

My husband, Bev, having been trained in forestry, has very definite ideas about trees and their comparative value. He has always considered the poplar to be a "weed" tree. Of course he tends to look at trees with an eye to their potential usefulness in one of his woodworking projects. My brothers and I always liked poplar trees when we were children. They were tall and slender and would sway gracefully in the wind to the accompaniment of the fluttering dance of myriads of pale green leaves….beautiful and perfect for climbing.

My Dad told my brother, Tom, and I about how he and his friends would sometimes chase one another through the treetops when they were children. He said they would climb the trees in a poplar grove and when you got up high enough you could set them swinging by throwing your weight from side to side. You had to get your tree to bend far enough to allow you to reach out and catch hold of the tree next to it.

Occasionally it would involve a bit of a jump but it was possible to swing from tree to tree eluding your pursuers without ever touching a foot to the ground. It was a mode of transportation that required a fair bit of agility not to mention nerves of steel. It was just the sort of game to appeal to boys growing up in the woods of Northern Ontario.

Eyes Wide Open

It sounded exciting to me but it also sounded dangerous, far too dangerous to tempt me into trying it for myself. I did climb trees but I kept my climbing confined to one single tree at a time, preferably one with reassuringly thick and sturdy branches. I had no illusions of being able to fly and I wanted no sudden encounters with thin air.

Not so my brother, Dave. He confessed recently that when he was in Grade 7 he discovered a stand of poplars in the forest near our home and decided to try a little treetop travel for himself. Perhaps he'd also heard my Dad speak of his childhood experiences. In any case, he chose a starting point and began to climb, pulling himself up from branch to increasingly slender branch until the whole tree began to bend and sway under his weight.

His first attempts to swing and catch hold of another tree were a bit clumsy but he eventually managed to get a firm grip with one hand while letting go with the other, transferring his weight to the new tree. Timing was critical but he kept practicing until he could move easily from tree to tree. It was an exhilarating experience, one that he wanted to share.

Eventually he talked one of his young friends into coming along to witness his newfound skill. His enthusiasm was contagious as he climbed the first tree and proceeded to demonstrate his technique. He swung mightily and made a grab for the tree next to the one he'd come up, snagging it on the first try as his friend stared up at him in wide-eyed wonder.

Eyes Wide Open

"See...it's easy!" he called down from his new perch with a grin stretching wide to reveal the gap in his two front teeth. "Come on!"

It only took moments for the other boy to climb the tree he'd just left. Dave moved on to the next tree and kept going, knowing that his friend would be following. Tarzan had nothing on the two of them, he thought, visions of monkeys dancing in his brain. A terrified shriek followed by the crash and snap of breaking branches somewhere behind him jerked him out of his pleasant daydream.

There was no response to his call and his vivid imagination flared to life with a picture of his friend lying broken and bleeding at the base of a poplar tree. Galvanized into action, he scrambled down, dropping from branch to branch, frantic to reach the ground. He jumped the last couple of feet and turned to push his way back through the undergrowth, terrified of what he would discover.

The angels must have been watching out for them that day. Dave's friend actually survived his fall with nothing worse than having the wind knocked out of him. He landed squarely in a patch of soft moss and that's where Dave found him gasping for air and surrounded by a litter of fallen twigs and leaves. It was the only spot in the entire area that was free of boulders and jagged outcrops of rock. They counted themselves more than lucky and decided to keep quiet about the whole thing. There's nothing like a near death experience to take the fun out of playing Tarzan.

Eyes Wide Open

Miss Independence

      I took a year off between High School and College. It was my chance to move away from home and become an independent adult. I decided I would go to Prince Edward Island and find a job in Charlottetown. My mother always referred to it as the time I ran away from home but I didn't see it that way. I was seventeen years old and very "responsible". I made arrangements to stay with a church family in Charlottetown and purchased my train ticket with the promise that if I didn't find a job within the first three weeks I'd return. I was fairly confident that wouldn't happen so it was an easy promise to make, especially since I could tell my parents were trying very hard to pretend that they weren't worried about me being on my own out there.

      As it turned out, they didn't need to worry. Within two days of my arrival I was able to find a job that included a place to live. I went to work almost immediately at Sunset Lodge, a Salvation Army home for elderly ladies. It was an old mansion converted into a retirement residence with two women officers from the Salvation Army to run the place and live on site. I had the top floor all to myself with a spacious room and a private bathroom. My job was to fill in for the kitchen and housekeeping staff on their days off. I would also be the staff member *in situ* whenever the Major and the Captain had to be away for meetings. It was a great job, almost like living with two mothers and twenty one grandmothers.

Eyes Wide Open

It was the first time in my life I was being treated as an adult and I wanted very much to earn their respect and prove that they'd not made a mistake in hiring me. After the first week I asked about doing my laundry and the cook told me there were big industrial machines in the cellar for doing the residents' laundry and all the linens and towels. For my own personal laundry I could use the smaller machine and hang my things on the clotheslines that were strung at one end of the room. I thanked her and made my way down carrying my basket and the soap I'd purchased on my day off.

I'd never been in this part of the basement before but I groped around until I found a switch and flicked on the overhead lights. I glanced at the big stainless steel washer and dryer. Next to them sat a long table with a basket of clothespins on a shelf above it. The lines were there and I looked around for the smaller machine I'd been told to use.

There it sat next to a couple of washtubs in the back corner...an ancient wringer washer. Did people actually still use the things? I had a vague memory of my mother using one when I was very young but that wouldn't help me much. There was absolutely no way I was going to march back upstairs in defeat, admitting that I didn't have a clue how to operate it. How hard could it be anyway?

I set the basket down and glanced over my shoulder to make sure no one was around before lifting the lid on the washer to have a peek inside. A thorough inspection of the rest of the machine gave me at least an idea of how it was supposed to work. It had two on/off switches, one on the

Eyes Wide Open

wringer itself and one on the body of the washer. The second one had to work the agitator. There was a hose clipped to the outside that could be unclipped and fed into a bucket for draining. I found another hose that I could attach to the tap to use to fill it.

I plugged it in to test the switches and smiled in satisfaction when they did exactly what I suspected they would. I found a little lever and discovered that it would allow the wringer to swing around to 90 degrees. That would solve the problem of rinsing. I could fill the machine to wash the clothes and then run them through the wringer and into the washtub filled with cold water to rinse them by hand. Then I could swing the wringer around to run them through from the rinse to the empty washtub before hanging them. Satisfied that I had it sorted out correctly I set about to do my first wash, inordinately pleased that I hadn't had to confess my ignorance and ask for help.

Two sweating hours later I was ready to kick the confounded thing to China and back. Two of my nightgowns had inexplicably gotten tangled in the wringers and by the time I'd managed to free them they looked like they'd been chewed up by an army of starving mice. My favourite sweater came through the other side all right but the sleeves ended up six inches longer than when I'd started. I tried putting it in the industrial dryer in the hopes that it would shrink but it was a long shot that didn't pay off.

At least I got the job done with all my fingers intact. Obviously, this new/old way of doing the wash was going

Eyes Wide Open

to take a lot of practice. I carried my basket back upstairs with my chin high and a pained smile for the cook as I passed the kitchen. I never admitted to a soul that I'd had a problem but I did wonder if I might have saved my clothes a beating if I'd asked for a little help after all. Perhaps there was such a thing as being too independent….or too proud….or both.

Eyes Wide Open

A Child's Perspective

  Bev spent some years as a Dairy Herdsman when our children were preschoolers. We lived on the farm where he worked so it was the next best thing to having a farm of our own. Lauren was still a baby but the boys often went to the barn with their Dad to watch him work and to see the animals. They learned to be careful not to ride their tricycles too close to the gutters and to stay out of the way whenever the cows were being moved. If they were lucky one of the barn cats would have kittens that they could catch and play with.

  There was no bull on the farm. The cows were artificially inseminated when the time came for them to be bred. The vet would come at a later date and do a check to confirm the pregnancy. He would pull on a shoulder length glove and lift the cow's tail to one side so that he could slip his hand (and most of his arm) into the cow's vagina to do a manual examination. No one paid much attention to two goggle-eyed little boys watching from the sidelines.

  I came into the kitchen on a day soon after one such visit to find Jason down on his hands and knees, mooing plaintively. Daniel had one arm encased in the plastic sleeve that the newspaper came in and he was poking his brother in the behind. I halted just inside the doorway and stared.

  "What are you doing?" I demanded. I thought I could make a pretty accurate guess but I was curious about how they would explain it. I kept my face carefully neutral as Daniel straightened up and turned to me.

"I'm the vet," he announced. "I'm checking for poop."

"I see," I nodded, my cheeks stiff with the effort not to laugh. "Well, carry on then."

Obviously they'd drawn their own conclusions about the mysterious activity they had witnessed. I decided to let Bev handle the explanations. No wonder farm children learn about the birds and the bees at such a young age.

Eyes Wide Open

The Swimming Hole

My Dad spent some of his childhood living with his family in a log cabin built back in the woods in Northern Ontario. The house was a long way from the nearest road and had to be reached by hiking along a trail through the forest. Supplies were carried in on a toboggan in winter and in huge backpacks in summer. He and his brothers and sisters made their own entertainment when they weren't occupied in the many chores necessary to the family's survival.

They were delighted the summer they discovered a beaver pond that was deep enough to swim in. Unfortunately, their first attempt at using it as a swimming hole revealed one major flaw. It turned out to be infested with leeches. There are few things more horrifying than emerging from the water covered in clinging three inch long bloodsuckers that refuse to let go unless you happen to have a handful of salt or a lit cigarette to burn them off. No one was keen to try it a second time but my Dad and his brothers refused to be put off. They were determined to make the pond their own. All it would need was guts, perseverance and a little ingenuity….no problem.

They "borrowed" the axe to cut down a few trees and went to work constructing a raft. It wasn't long before they had something big enough to carry them and they lost no time in trying out the plan they'd worked out to clear the pond of leeches. Armed with a bucket they poled themselves out into the centre of the open water. With

Eyes Wide Open

infinite caution they inched their way to one side of the raft tipping it just enough so that the water would slosh around their ankles on that side. The last thing they wanted was to have it flip right over dumping them all in the drink.

Once they had the raft balanced with one side underwater all they had to do was wait. They might as well have rung a dinner bell with their own feet as the main course. In moments the water covering the raft was black with leeches. On a prearranged signal, the boys would redistribute their weight and the raft would bob back to the surface leaving the leeches stranded on the logs. Then all that was left was to collect them in the bucket before setting the trap again. What do you do with a bucket full of leeches? In the end they decided to build a fire and burn them to ensure they couldn't somehow find their way back into the water.

It took countless repetitions over the next weeks until they began to notice a lessening in the numbers of leeches they caught in that way. Eventually they could stand ankle deep on one side of the raft without enticing a single leech to the proffered feast. It was a victory of sorts. The pond was pronounced safe to swim in at last. They still had to contend with an occasional bloodsucker but after all they'd gone through it seemed a small inconvenience rather than any sort of deterrent to their fun. The Beaver Pond was rechristened the Swimming Hole and for the rest of the summer echoed with the sounds of children at play.

Eyes Wide Open

One of a Kind

Not long ago I had a chat with a fellow whose hobby it is to restore rare old cars. He spends years searching out parts and thousands of dollars rebuilding a car from bottom up. The end result is a beautiful automobile that looks like it just came from the factory…a real treasure. I've noticed that a lot of men like to express themselves in the cars they drive. My son wanted a truck, not because he really needed a truck but because he felt it said something about who he is. Custom features, detailing, even color can be and often are an expression of the owner's personality.

Of course some cars seem to have a personality of their own. That was certainly true of the old Volkswagen that my friend, Don, drove back in the late seventies. It was a Beetle with a big heart and enough eccentricities to keep life interesting. Come to think of it, the same thing could probably have been said about Don. The car was easily recognizable even from a distance. Not only was it red, it was almost completely covered in bumper stickers that were slapped on like haphazard band aids proclaiming the slogans of the Jesus Generation to the world. My mother was always acutely embarrassed whenever he parked it in our driveway. My friends and I would all pile in and Don would drive off waving to the neighbors as we passed. I have to admit we enjoyed the stares and raised eyebrows.

We travelled a lot of miles in that old car. With a little judicious squeezing and stacking we could fit seven passengers in it and still leave Don enough room to handle

Eyes Wide Open

the stick shift. Breathing was a little difficult but over the short haul it was doable. We even did some occasional off-roading. The old girl was tough enough to handle driving down the steps in Bell Park without the wheels falling off and if we did happen to sink to the axels driving up the side of a sand pit, there were usually enough of us to lift her out.

We never had an actual breakdown that I can remember but there were plenty of quirks that made driving a bit interesting. Don was the only one who could manage it. The gas pedal tended to stick from time to time so he had to drive with no shoe on his right foot. That way he could curl his toes around the end of the pedal and pull it up if he had to. The heater only seemed to work in summer and sometimes it just refused to turn off. Good thing the windows didn't stick.

Driving in the rain could also be a problem since the windshield wipers were a trifle uncoordinated. They would start out keeping time well enough but before long they would begin to operate independent of each other. Their smooth side to side motion would become more and more disjointed until inevitably they would meet in the middle and come to a shuddering stop, hopelessly tangled. Don would smack his fist against the inside of the window and that would be enough to shake them free of each other to start the dance all over again. If he hit the window too hard they would spring apart with such force that they ended up standing straight up in the air and waving about like disconnected eyebrows until someone rolled a window down far enough to reach out and pull them back to rest on the glass once more.

Eyes Wide Open

In the winter the defroster would only clear a spot about the size of a coaster in the bottom left corner of the windshield. Don would drive all hunched over, peering out through that little peephole and it was the job of whoever was riding shotgun to ply the scraper in an attempt to clear the rest of the window to enlarge the view. Ah, so many fond memories!

Eventually, the Beetle went the way of the Dodo and we all moved on. We grew and changed and the things that are expressions of who we are changed with us. These days Don is driving a Jaguar and that fits perfectly in the world of finance that has become his milieu. Still, I have no doubt that there is still a small part of him that wouldn't mind driving down some stairs in a beat up Volkswagen Beetle just for old time's sake.

Eyes Wide Open

Runaway Horses

The harvest is nearly done for this year apart from a few acres of corn still drying on the stalks. I can watch the progression of the season every time I glance out my windows at the fields surrounding our home. My children used to love watching the big tractors and wagons trundling past the perimeter of our yard on their circuit of the neighboring farm. They learned early on to recognize the different equipment used to plant, cultivate and harvest various crops. Farming has come a long way since our parents' time.

Back in the forties when my parents were on a small farm in Northern Ontario, they still worked with horses. Getting hay into the barn was a labor intensive proposition. First it had to be cut, then raked into windrows and finally loaded onto a wagon with pitchforks. Of course the load would then have to be forked into the barn. I believe my mother was still in her teens the year she had a little accident with the dump rake.

If you were operating a dump rake pulled by horses you would sit perched on a seat between a widely spaced set of two big wheels with the rake itself behind you. Your job would be to drive the horses up and down the field while the rake caught the hay up in its huge curving tines. When it was full there was a foot pedal that would lift the rake to dump its load before continuing on. The trick was to dump each load in line with the one beside it so that a fairly straight windrow was created. The wagon could then

Eyes Wide Open

be driven slowly along each windrow while the hay was loaded.

Mom sat clutching the reigns in both hands as she slowly drove the rake across the field with her friend, Mary, walking alongside to keep her company. No one knows for sure what caused the horses to spook. Perhaps one of them got stung by a bee. In the blink of an eye their placid, tail-swishing plod became a confused jangle of stamping hooves and tossing heads. Mom was struggling to get the team under control when they bolted. She was thrown completely out of the seat and fell to the ground still grasping the reigns so that she was being dragged just in front of the arcing tines of the rake.

Mary screamed and kept on screaming, which did not have a particularly calming effect on the runaway horses. Mom had no thought to spare for her friend. She knew with a sickening certainty that if she let go of the reigns it would mean getting caught in the rake as it was hauled over her by the fleeing team. She held on with a desperation born of fear as she was bounced across the rough stubble of the hay field with the rake looming over her. It was one of those situations where every second lasts an age. With the horses showing no signs of slowing she could feel her last strength draining away and she knew she couldn't hold on any longer.

She closed her eyes as the reigns slipped out of her grasping fingers, convinced she was about to be mangled terribly. At that precise moment the tongue broke with a splintering crack, the jagged end catching in the dry earth

Eyes Wide Open

and flipping the entire rake up and over to land upside down on the backs of the two horses. It stopped them cold and they stood sweating and trembling, shocked into immobility.

It took a few moments for help to arrive, enough time for Mom to realize that she wasn't dead after all. When she finally understood what actually happened she couldn't believe how lucky she'd been. The timing was incredible. The whole thing could have ended very badly but apart from scrapes and bruises she came out of it all in one piece. I'm not so sure about luck though. I've always believed it was a miracle.

Eyes Wide Open

The Paper Trail

This week I bought eight double rolls of Pepto-Bismol pink toilet paper in support of the Canadian Breast Cancer Association. It catches me by surprise each time I step into the bathroom. That hot, bright splash of color fairly jumps off the wall in the otherwise neutral palette that I usually prefer. I find it a bit distracting not to mention unnerving to use something that looks like cotton candy for the purpose for which it was actually intended. Still, my mother went through breast cancer twice so I tend to try to put up with the pink in order to show my support.

There are things more important than color when it comes to toilet paper. My personal pet peeve is that scratchy, insubstantial excuse for paper that you sometimes find in public washrooms. It is generally wound so tight on the industrial size roll that it is impossible to pull off more than one square at a time without tearing it….very annoying. Of course there are occasions when encountering a better quality of toilet paper can have its own set of problems.

My parents were on their way to a follow up appointment in Toronto after my mother's first bout with breast cancer. Neither of them felt particularly at ease in the city so rather than leaving their planned route to the clinic in order to find a place to eat they decided to stop at a hotel they passed and eat lunch in the restaurant there. They entered the hotel and Mom stopped to use the restroom before they went on into the dining room. Dad

Eyes Wide Open

agreed to wait for her at the entrance on the far side of the lobby.

The bathroom was lovely but every woman knows how challenging it can be to manage in the close confines of a stall that is only two and a half feet wide especially if you are wearing a bulky winter coat. In the end she got herself sorted out and made her way to the sink to wash her hands. She failed to notice that she had somehow caught the end of the toilet paper in her clothing and it was trailing out from under her coat. Completely oblivious, she made her way out to the lobby and started walking across to where Dad was waiting. There was a lull in the conversation at the front desk as she passed. She couldn't understand why everyone seemed to be looking at her.

Dad took a couple of hurried steps in her direction, his face a study in horrified embarrassment.

"What's that?" he whispered urgently.

"What?" Mom demanded, truly bewildered by all the attention.

He pointed behind her and she turned to see a 50 foot long trail of toilet paper beginning somewhere under her coat and reaching all the way across the hotel lobby, under the restroom door and back to where it appeared she was still tethered to the roll in the stall she had occupied moments before. No problems with premature tearing there. It looked as though the whole roll would follow her

Eyes Wide Open

no matter how many doors she went through. She snatched it free and dropped it as though it was burning her fingers.

One look into each other's eyes and the unspoken message, "Let's get out of here!" came through loud and clear. They abandoned all thoughts of lunch and hurried out to the parking lot, eager to escape the grinning faces of the staff at the hotel's reception desk.

That little incident turned out to be a blessing in disguise. Whatever nervousness Mom had been feeling about her appointment was completely eclipsed by their experience in the hotel. It was like an episode of the "I Love Lucy Show". No wonder everyone laughed. Once they were safely hidden away in their car Mom and Dad thought it was funny too. She could hardly wait to get home and tell us all about the paper trail she'd left behind.

Eyes Wide Open

Filleted

I went to a Japanese restaurant once with my brother, Richard, and his wife, June. It was a night to remember for a small town girl. We found ourselves seated with about five other patrons, all of us ranged in a semicircle around a grill that was built right into the table. Each table had its own chef and the food was cooked right there in front of you. The chefs didn't just cook, they made it an art. Everything was done with a flourish. Knives were flipped and tossed, vegetables juggled and chopped, seasonings flicked from a spoon held high in the air to arc gracefully down on the food below, and everything done at lightning speed to produce dishes that were both beautiful and delicious. It was one of the most memorable dining experiences I've ever had.

Richard loves to cook and produces some amazing meals of his own. Even when they are camping or out sailing, he and June eat very well. Years ago they went on a camping trip where they canoed to a remote site in one of our Provincial Parks. They took their time setting everything up. The spot they'd chosen was remote enough to be entirely private and the weather was all anyone could ask for.

Richard caught some fish and decided to cook them right then and there. What could be better than fresh fish fried over an open fire? He got the fire going and went to work with his filleting knife while June continued to put their tent in order.

Eyes Wide Open

The sun was shining overhead and Richard was whistling while he worked. They'd left the cares and stresses of a hectic life behind and it was going to be a great weekend. In an excess of good feeling he tossed the knife with a flourish that would have rivaled anything we saw in that Japanese restaurant.

Perhaps it was not the wisest thing to do when the ground underfoot is as treacherous as the rock he was squatting on at the time. A filleting knife has a long narrow blade that is of necessity extremely sharp. A slip, a fumble, and in the blink of an eye the prospects for the weekend took a drastic turn for the worse. He stabbed himself…in the butt.

June stuck her head out of the tent when the whistling was abruptly cut off to be replaced by a muffled curse. Richard was carefully extracting the knife from where it protruded from his outraged backside.

"What happened?" she demanded, hurrying over to assess the damage.

"I lost my balance," he muttered. "I guess I fell on it."

I suppose if you are going to stab yourself with a filleting knife, the *gluteus maximus* is not a bad place to do it - nothing vital lurking under the surface. There wasn't even much blood. The knife had gone straight in so the wound was small but deep. They cleaned and bandaged it as best they could and decided they would be wise to head

Eyes Wide Open

to the nearest emergency room. The combination of a dirty knife and minimal first aid made infection a near certainty. Of course, getting to a hospital was not a simple matter when you were camping in a remote site and your car was hours away by canoe.

With no other choice the camp was dismantled and packed in record time. Richard hobbled around trying to help and eventually they were loaded and launched. He paddled the whole way back perched precariously on one cheek. By the time they reached the car and ultimately the hospital his entire leg had stiffened up and he thought he would give up sitting for good.

The emergency room was crowded when they arrived and he limped to the desk to register. The triage nurse began her assessment with a question or two about his presenting problem. He glanced over his shoulder at the assorted people filling the chairs in the waiting room and leaned in to speak in a low undertone that couldn't be overheard.

"Excuse me, I didn't catch what you said," she offered with an apologetic smile.

He looked around once more, raised a hand to partially cover his mouth and increased his volume just a notch in an attempt to explain without broadcasting his problem to the entire room.

"I beg your pardon?"

Eyes Wide Open

"I stabbed myself in the butt with a filleting knife!" he blurted, huffing in exasperation.

So much for discretion. Ah well, let them laugh. It was an altogether perfect ending to their aborted weekend. He supposed he deserved it.

Eyes Wide Open

Skunk Tales

Living in the country means dealing with an assortment of pesky creatures that are intent on foraging in vegetable gardens and garbage cans or building nests in the most inconvenient places. One morning we came out to find an entire section of our lawn chopped up as though someone had taken a hoe and hacked it to bits. I couldn't imagine why anyone would want to do such a thing. In the end it turned out that we had a resident skunk digging up the grass in search of grubs during the night. Neither of us was keen on having a skunk as a close neighbor so Bev set out a live trap to see if we could capture it.

It was only a matter of time before the furry little fumigator followed his nose to the bait in the trap and ended up caught. Bev's theory was that if you covered the cage so the skunk couldn't see you, it wouldn't feel any need to spray in self-defense. Deciding to put it to the test, he crept cautiously forward with an old blanket held out in front of him like a shield. He managed to get close enough to toss it so that its folds settled in a haphazard cloud completely covering both cage and occupant in shadowy darkness. He then picked the whole thing up and, careful to make no sudden moves, carried it to the back of the truck with the intent of driving it off to some distant field where the luckless captive could be released with no chance of finding its way back to our house.

The theory proved sound as the skunk showed no signs of agitation and endured the entire trip without

Eyes Wide Open

resorting to its only effective weapon. Bev positioned the covered trap so that the skunk would emerge downwind of him, lifted the edge of the blanket just enough to open the door from behind, and then beat a hasty retreat. He watched from a safe distance until the little creature finally decided it was safe to emerge and waddled off into the distance.

That particular incident ended with the sweet smell of success. My Dad told a different story about one of his own boyhood encounters. He and a chum were walking to school when they noticed a skunk wandering about in the yard of a neighboring farm. School was forgotten with the prospect of much more interesting fun near at hand. The farm was quiet with no signs that anyone was stirring in the house or barn.

They set their lunches on the porch in order to arm themselves with the only weapons at hand, a broom and the galvanized zinc washtub they found hanging from a nail on the outside wall. The big square tub was an essential piece of equipment that was a part of every household. It was used for any number of things - from laundry to bathing children to carrying vegetables from the garden to the root cellar during harvest time. I am quite certain that it had never been used for the purpose it would soon be employed in.

The boys set about stalking their prey with as much stealth as any big game hunter. They weren't total fools. The skunk might not be deadly but it was dangerous all the same and what they were doing was risky. Hearts pounding, they managed to edge close enough to make their move. The time for caution was past. Dad darted forward and, quick as a flash, trapped the unsuspecting skunk beneath the overturned washtub. Not to be outdone, his friend rushed in to give the tub a few good whacks with the broom.

Bev's theory definitely did not apply when the skunk happened to be trapped under a galvanized zinc washtub that was being energetically thumped with a wooden broom handle. Predictably, it let loose with its full arsenal and the boys leaped away in alarm when the spray hit the inside of the tub so that the pungent smell came wafting out from under the edges.

There was an outraged shout from the house and they looked up to see the farmer's wife scowling at them from the front porch where she had emerged to check on the commotion in the yard. She shook a fist at them and they did the only prudent thing in the circumstances. They made a run for it.

The boys never heard how the skunk eventually got released from its makeshift prison. They had no idea whether or not the washtub could ever again be used for laundering clothes or babies. They judged it best to steer clear of that particular farm for the foreseeable future. Their lost lunches caused a pang or two of regret but neither of them felt inclined to try to retrieve them. All things considered, it seemed a small price to pay.

Eyes Wide Open

A Lemon of a Pie

I don't really enjoy cooking but I do love to eat. That's always been a great incentive to me when it comes to getting supper on the table. Occasionally, I'll get a craving for a certain kind of food and that will be enough to set me searching through cook books to see just how complicated it would be to make. If the instructions alone are not enough to cure my desire to taste something new, I might actually give it a try.

Not all of my attempts are successful. The food, even though it may taste fine, rarely turns out looking anything like it does in the mouth watering pictures that tempted me in the first place. I also find it hard to reconcile that there are actually times when, in spite of the fact that I have followed the recipe religiously, the results are a total disaster. We'll say nothing about my ill-fated attempt at something called Buckaroo Beans...not even the dog would eat them.

I usually do all right with pies thanks to my mother's recipe for Never Fail Pie Crust. It lives up to its name for the most part and is relatively simple to make. In the second year of our marriage, Bev and I were living in Jamaica and he mentioned that lemon meringue had to be his all time favorite when it came to pies. One day I stumbled across a mix for lemon pie filling that was half hidden on an upper shelf at the local grocery store and I decided to buy it and surprise him by making one for dessert that night.

Eyes Wide Open

Bev was out for the afternoon so I set to work in high spirits. The Never Fail Pie Crust rolled out beautifully and I gently placed it in the pie plate, fluting the edges artistically and pricking it with a fork before popping it into the oven to bake. In the meantime I followed the directions on the box to make the filling on the stove top. I had to pause in my stirring to take the crust out of the oven and that was the first intimation that my project was not destined to go smoothly. My once beautiful crust had shrunk so that it only reached halfway up the sides of the pan, the fluted edges shriveled to indistinct lumps. There was no time to mourn though. I was supposed to stir the filling until it thickened and I didn't want to scorch it.

Twenty minutes later I was still stirring. The lemony concoction in the pot was bubbling softly but it still showed little or no sign of the promised thickening. I began to speculate on the actual age of the mix I'd purchased or the possible effects of Jamaica's hot and humid climate on the making of lemon pie. Finally, I decided to just go for it in the hopes that it would thicken as it cooled. I poured it into my diminished pie crust, careful not to overflow the edges. It was going to be a thin pie. I took out some of my frustration in beating the egg whites to stiff peaks for the meringue. Once it was spooned on and the whole thing baked, I set it to cool. I watched it closely but as the afternoon wore on hope faded.

Bev arrived to find me in tears. The pie sat on the counter, the meringue floating on the lemony soup beneath it. I wanted nothing more than to throw the whole mess over the fence out back. The disappointment was acute.

Eyes Wide Open

Bev, however, was not about to give up his lemon pie without a fight. I watched in amazement as he carefully slid the meringue from the top of the pie onto a plate. Then he poured the filling back into a pot to reheat. A few tablespoons of cornstarch had it thickened up in no time. Now why didn't I think of that! Once he had it back in the pie he simply slid the meringue back to its original place on top and pronounced it ready to eat.

It wasn't pretty. In fact it was a lemon of a pie altogether. Even so, we ate the whole thing. Since then Bev has had to settle for apple pie when I want to surprise him with a treat. He assures me that apple is his all time second favorite when it comes to pies. He can always have the lemon when we go out.

<u>Never Fail Pie Crust</u>
4 ½ c. flour
1 lb. shortening or lard
1 tsp. salt
¼ tsp. baking soda
1 egg
1 tsp. vinegar
Sift salt and soda into flour. Mix shortening through flour. To 1 egg in measuring cup add vinegar and make up to ¾ c. with cold water. Mix and chill. Roll out.

Eyes Wide Open

Have Bus Will Travel

On one of our trips this past summer we came across two elderly gentlemen in a campsite near ours. They had converted an old horse trailer into a camper by building a couple of cots inside and adding some shelving to store their supplies. They say that necessity is the mother of invention. Certainly, in my family there has always been a "do-it-yourself" mentality seasoned with both imagination and ingenuity. We often made do with homemade versions of those things that were beyond the reach of our limited pocketbooks.

That was how we came to be the proud owners of our own version of a Winnebago, the latest in RV's back in the early 70's. When my brother, Richard, heard about an old school bus that was for sale he immediately saw the potential. It was a short bus, only half the size of the regular buses that we rode to school every weekday. It had been sitting unused for some time so he got it for a very good price. He reckoned that with my Dad's help they could really make something of it and so in due time it ended up in our yard.

They spent the whole summer on the project. The first order of business was to strip all the seats out of it. The floor was then covered with linoleum and bunk beds long enough to accommodate the tall men in our family were built along both sides at the back with a curtain that could be drawn across in front of them for privacy. The top bunks were set on hinges so that they could be lowered to transform the beds into two couches facing each other across the centre aisle.

Two of the original seats were reinstalled with a table between them. It looked like a restaurant booth set just behind the driver's seat. They built cupboards along the opposite side to hold the camp stove, ice box and other supplies. It may not have had running water or a bathroom but by the time they were done it could pass for a cottage on wheels. They painted the outside grey and added some detailing in black to spruce it up and give it a whole new look. We thought it was gorgeous.

It did have a few drawbacks though. The first time we took it out on the road we discovered that with most of the seats removed there wasn't enough weight to smooth out the ride. Every bump was magnified to such a degree that anything not tied down got bounced all over the bus. That included us. Any encounter with a pothole would see us lifted right out of our seats to land on the floor if we weren't holding on for dear life. We also took to joking about our gas mileage being measured in gallons per mile instead of the other way around.

Nevertheless, Richard and some friends drove that bus all the way to Mexico and back and pronounced the trip a great success even though they ended up having to replace all the old tires before they got halfway. When they finally reached their destination the geriatric bus coughed out its last gasp and they began to think they would have to abandon it in Mexico. Richard managed to find a mechanic who promised to completely rebuild the engine for a ridiculously low price and they decided to take a chance on him. Never was a hundred dollars better spent. By the time he was done with it the engine had a whole new lease on life. The journey back to Canada went without a hitch.

Ultimately, the bus got retired in our backyard and became a sort of guest house. My younger brother, Tom, and I would have friends over to hang out and sleep in the bus and the novelty of it never wore off. It may not have been much fun to ride in but we thought it first rate as accommodations. It was one of a kind, better than a real Winnebago in my mind. It had Landry stamped all over it.

Eyes Wide Open

Brownie

Our dog, Brownie, came to live with us when our children were just about ready to start school. She was barely more than a pup herself at the time and it wasn't long before she became an important member of our family. She was a border collie/miniature collie cross which meant she was both smart and protective. Her previous owners had moved into town and were looking for a place in the country for her. I happened to be visiting them and mentioned that we were looking for a dog something like her. In moments the deal was done.

I paid close attention as they outlined the important lessons that they had already taught her. Apparently we wouldn't need to tie her unless we were going to be away for more than a day. If we told her to "guard the house" as we were leaving she would wait there patiently until we returned. She was accustomed to living outside, snug in her insulated dog house even in winter. We were told that if we did bring her into the house she had been taught to stay out of the rooms with carpet on the floor.

On the day she arrived we walked her all around the perimeter of the property to show her the limits of her new territory and she seemed to understand. She accepted her new circumstances eagerly enough and adopted us as though she'd been born at our house. She took her job as protector of the property very seriously though I suspect it was me and the children she was looking after rather than our worldly goods. She became a constant companion on

Eyes Wide Open

many adventures. Once the boys started school she would wait with them at the end of the driveway every morning till the school bus took them away. The end of the day would find her sitting back in that same spot staring up the road watching for their return.

We discovered she was terrified of thunderstorms and so there were times when she slept in the kitchen rather than the back yard. Eventually, she spent as much time inside as out. She never made a nuisance of herself by coming to the table when we were eating and, true to her early training, she kept strictly to the bare floors in the kitchen and the laundry room next to it. She wasn't pampered but she was definitely loved.

Brownie was a hunter at heart. Grandpa Livingston would invite us to visit if we'd bring her along to help him hunt coons in the cornfield. She actually turned out to be a good coon dog. She was less successful when chasing squirrels or rabbits or even deer. She would tear off in enthusiastic pursuit, her frenzied barking pitched high with excitement even though she never managed to catch one. Groundhogs were much easier prey. If she caught one of them out in the open the outcome was inevitable. We would come across the gruesome remains of a partially eaten carcass on the front lawn and someone would have to fetch a shovel to give it a hasty burial somewhere far enough from the house to avoid having it dragged back the next day. She also caught more mice than our cat ever did.

She was in the house with me one winter day when I pulled open the drawer in the bottom of my stove to

Eyes Wide Open

discover that a mouse had filled it with dryer lint and built a nest among my baking tins. Horrors! I could feel my skin crawl at the thought of what might be lurking under all that fluff. Much as I wanted to, I couldn't just close the drawer again and pretend I hadn't seen anything. I was going to have to deal with it so I steeled my nerves and leaned down to shout a challenge into the pie plates in the hopes that any resident mouse would die of a heart attack before I uncovered it. I kicked the drawer a few times for good measure and then Brownie sat watching with head cocked to one side as I used a pair of tongs to reach in and gingerly pull the pans out one at a time.

I'd almost reached the bottom when a terrified mouse shot out from under the stove and skittered across the kitchen floor. I dropped the tongs and jumped to one side nearly tripping over the stack of pans I'd piled there.

"Get it, Brownie!" I shrieked.

She'd already seen it and the chase was on. Chaos ensued with the mouse finally racing straight into the living room to disappear under the couch. Brownie skidded to an undignified halt at the edge of the carpet and even with me jumping up and down crying, "The rules are off!" she refused to cross over into forbidden territory. She just turned her reproachful eyes on me and I could almost hear her thinking, "you're trying to trick me aren't you?"

I sighed in defeat and went to fetch the broom. I was going to have to get this mouse the hard way. Furniture got shoved here and there as I chased that pesky rodent around the living room with Brownie watching intently and barking encouragement from the sidelines. It was hopeless.

      The mouse got away and I tried to console myself with the thought that perhaps the whole experience was so traumatic for it that it would leave the house altogether and never return. Even so, I found a new home for my baking tins and for the rest of the winter the drawer in the bottom of the stove stayed empty except for the mouse trap we set there. Brownie had to content herself with hunting outside. At least there were no carpets out there to spoil her fun.

Eyes Wide Open

Catch a Beaver by the Tail

My Dad was always full of stories and no matter how far-fetched they sounded we believed them absolutely. After all, we knew him. He talked about killing spruce hens with a slingshot to save ammunition when he was a boy, and teasing trout out of the river with his bare hands. He maintained that if you could catch a beaver by the tail and lift its hind legs off the ground you could walk it around like a wheelbarrow and it wouldn't be able to turn and bite you. Heaven only knows how he discovered that one to be true! My brother, Tom, discovered first hand that it was no idle claim. He told the story himself at my Dad's memorial service and I will repeat it now.

Tom was about 16 years old and he and Dad were on a five day canoe trip down the Spanish River in Northern Ontario. The trip itself was a wilderness adventure with plenty of rapids to run, some of them quite challenging. At one point they put in to shore in a small cove where there was a stream running down into the river. Dad spotted a beaver in the woods and his face lit up with mischief.

He gripped Tom's shoulder and propelled him toward the stream. "Stand just there, with one leg on either side of the water," he instructed.

"What for?" Tom queried suspiciously even as he moved to obey.

Eyes Wide Open

Dad's instructions were brief and concise. "I'm going to circle around and get that beaver moving. He'll come straight down the stream heading for the deeper water in the river and when he passes between your legs, reach down and grab him by the tail."

Tom's eyebrows rose nearly to his hairline and his mouth dropped open.

"Make sure you get his hind legs up off the ground," Dad called over his shoulder. "That way he won't be able to reach around and bite you."

Tom stood where he'd been placed, his mind racing furiously. There's no way I'm doing this, he thought.

In moments Dad was back. "Here he comes! Get ready now!" he urged.

Sure enough, the beaver was coming straight down the stream. Instinct took over and Tom, his nerve breaking, scrambled frantically out of the way at the last minute. Dad jumped in to take his place and when the beaver tried to get past him, he reached down and caught hold of the broad tail with both hands. With one heave he raised the back end of that beaver off the ground and it instantly became apparent that the awkward position rendered it completely helpless. Dad started to walk it down to the river bank with Tom running alongside. It really was like pushing a wheelbarrow after all.

Eyes Wide Open

Once they'd reached the shore Dad encouraged Tom to hold on to the beaver's tail himself for a few moments. It wasn't as easy as it looked. Beavers are heavy and this one never once stopped scrabbling with its front paws in a futile attempt to get to the river. Nevertheless, Tom actually got to experience holding a beaver by the tail. How many people can say that?

"Okay, you can let him go now," Dad finally decided.

Tom released his hold and the beaver made a dash to safety, disappearing into the water almost immediately. He and Dad just stood there grinning at one another, savoring the moment. It was an experience to treasure and remember.

Tom has told the story often and he says that most people don't really believe it. That doesn't bother him though. He might not have believed it himself if he hadn't been standing there on the shore that day with the muddy imprint of wet beaver tail still smudging the palms of his hands.

Eyes Wide Open

Needled

  I'm not much for wearing jewelry so I never felt a need to have my ears pierced as a girl. Why on earth would I want someone to poke a hole through my earlobe just so I could wear earrings? My friend, Karen, was always trying to talk me into having it done when we were in college but the whole idea made me cringe. I did not like needles.

  She and I were nursing students back in the 70's and it wasn't long before she pointed out that I was going to have to get over my gut reaction to needles. Like it or not, I was eventually going to have to stick one into a patient and it wasn't likely to inspire confidence if I looked terrified at the prospect. We learned all about the safe handling of needles and syringes in class and we studied all the theory regarding the giving of injections.

  Volunteers willing to let us practice on them were a bit scarce on the ground. In fact they were non-existent so we had to practice by injecting an orange until it was ready to burst. We also spent a lot of time stabbing mattresses to get a feel for the force we imagined you would need to exert when working with a human subject. Ultimately, we would just have to learn by doing it.

  How well I remember the first time I actually had to give a shot to the patient I was caring for. As students we wore conspicuous yellow uniforms and our name tags clearly identified us as nurses in training. There was no

Eyes Wide Open

possible chance that our amateur status might be missed or overlooked.

"You've done this before have you?" my prospective victim asked with a dubious look at the loaded syringe I was carrying on a little tray when I approached the bed.

"Of course," I replied with a bright smile that I hoped would disguise my nervousness.

I felt it would be unwise to confess that my only subjects to date had been inanimate objects. Luckily, the patient was facing the other way and couldn't see my face at the crucial moment. I managed to avoid verbalizing the litany of "3...2...1...fire" that was sounding in my head at the time. I gave that injection like a pro and was vastly pleased when he insisted that he hadn't felt a thing.

It wasn't long before both Karen and I were able to give injections with a confidence that no longer had to be feigned. I certainly grew more comfortable with needles than I'd ever been before. Perhaps that was why Karen thought it a good time to renew her campaign to get me to agree to have my ears pierced. She even offered to do it for me. She insisted it couldn't be much different than giving an injection after all. She figured she could use a couple of pre-packaged sterile needles from the hospital just to be on the safe side. It wouldn't cost a thing but the price of the earrings. She was a little startled when I finally agreed to let her do it. She didn't back down though and we set about making our plans.

Eyes Wide Open

The following Saturday found me perched on a chair in the middle of Karen's living room. She carefully marked a dot on each earlobe to make sure the holes would be evenly spaced. Then we pinched my ear between a couple of ice cubes and held it that way for as long as I could stand it. It was supposed to be anesthetic of a sort. Once my ear was thoroughly numbed with cold she opened the needle packet and stood poised in front of me for several long seconds.

"What are you waiting for?" I asked.

"I don't want to hurt you," she admitted.

"You said this wasn't going to hurt," I accused.

She pasted on the bright smile I recognized as the same one we used when we were trying to convince a patient that we knew what we were doing. I can't say I found it very reassuring. Before I could change my mind about the whole thing however, she deftly plunged the needle through my earlobe and stepped back leaving it in place.

"You were right," I marveled. "It didn't hurt!"

We went through the whole process once more with the other ear and I was sitting there like some African tribesman with two 22 gauge, 1 ½ inch needles sticking through my earlobes when Karen's husband, Don, walked in. He took one look, turned a little pale, and marched straight through to the bedroom with his gaze averted.

Eyes Wide Open

"I'm not even going to ask," he muttered as he swept past. "Just let me know when it's over."

All in all, the piercing went well. It was when we tried to put the earrings in that we ran into trouble. It seems they were just slightly bigger than the holes they were expected to go through. That was where anesthetic would have been useful. We were fresh out of bright ideas so we ended up using brute force to push them through…a most unpleasant experience. Karen hated doing it even more than I hated having it done.

The venture was eventually pronounced a qualified success in spite of the difficulties. The earrings were in at last and Don was given the okay to emerge from the bedroom. Karen discovered that piercing ears was not for the faint of heart. I was her first and last customer. The do-it-yourself home piercing kit should have included nerves of steel…and bigger ice cubes.

Eyes Wide Open

Tagging Along

My daughter, Lauren, and her husband, Andrew, are lovers of all things outdoors. When they had a baby they were determined that it would not mean giving up the camping and canoeing that they so enjoyed. They bought an infant life jacket for their baby daughter, Rea, and plan to carry on with their adventures as a family. That prospect might sound intimidating to some parents but it isn't impossible. It's just the sort of thing my own parents might have decided.

We rarely got left behind when my Mom and Dad wanted to get out. In their early years of marriage they would sometimes go to a movie on a Friday night. They didn't have a car so my Dad would pedal the family to the theatre on his bicycle with my Mom perched sidesaddle on the crossbar and Richard, who was a baby at the time, in the basket out front.

By the time my younger brother, Tom, and I came along they had discovered Drive-In Theatres. When Friday night rolled around Dad would pull the mattress off of one of the beds and cram it into the back of our station wagon. We would head out to the Atomic Drive-In with Tom and I already dressed in our pajamas. We got to play on the swings and merry-go-round that were set up at the edge of the car park as long as we ran back to the car when it got dark enough for the movie to start.

Eyes Wide Open

When we got too tired to stay awake any longer we just curled up on the mattress and went to sleep. As we got older Dad dispensed with the mattress and we graduated to the back seat. Mom would always make us scrunch down and try to look small as we drove through the gate so she could still get the maximum discount for children.

Back in those days each parking spot at the Drive-In had a post with a speaker on a long cord that you would clip to the inside of your window for sound. Of course you couldn't roll the window up all the way and in Northern Ontario that meant you ran the risk of getting eaten by mosquitoes before the movie was half over. The management tried to combat the problem by "fogging" the lot during intermission. Someone wearing a contraption that looked like a flamethrower would wander up and down through the rows of cars blowing a billowing white cloud of fog out of the nozzle attached to the tanks on his back.

I shudder to think what sort of chemicals it might have contained. It certainly gave the whole place an air of mystery and perhaps it even helped control the bugs. If it was particularly bad Mom would light up a mosquito coil inside the car and set it on the dash. It's a wonder we didn't all choke but no one complained. It was all part of the fun. Dad would always buy us a hot dog or some other treat from the snack bar while we waited for the fog to clear and the movie to start again.

We saw a lot of movies that way. Movies like "Thoroughly Modern Millie" and "Lenington and the Ants". That last one may have traumatized me because I

Eyes Wide Open

remember it clearly in spite of how young I was. It was seriously scary with a massive swarm of African Fire Ants completely engulfing and eating anyone who stumbled into their path. At least we had the option of ducking down behind the seat if the action got too intense. As far as I know, neither of us grew up with an irrational fear of ants so I suppose it couldn't have been that bad.

Movies weren't the only outings we got to tag along on. When my parents went to a house party we went with them. I learned to polka by dancing in living rooms with my Dad. My mother was fond of playing Bingo and she often brought me along. She would give me one of her cards to play and watched like a hawk to make sure I didn't miss any numbers. I was always more fascinated by the strange array of good luck charms that some of the other players surrounded themselves with than I was with watching my card.

There were rabbit's foot key-chains, four leaf clovers, tiny figurines of all descriptions, even a turkey wishbone. As far as I could tell none of them made a bit of difference to whether people won or not. I never did care much for the game but I loved being with my Mom. She got so excited whenever she had a chance to shout Bingo or even when she came close to it that you couldn't help but get excited along with her. Her pleasure was contagious.

It didn't matter what the activity was. We got to participate and that made it special. We grew up knowing that our parents wanted us with them. That's probably why spending time together means so much to me now. I'm not

Eyes Wide Open

sure just how Lauren and Andrew will manage canoeing with a baby but I love the intent of their hearts in it. Rea will tag along with them just the way we did with our parents when we were children. I wouldn't trade those times for anything.

Eyes Wide Open

The Night before Christmas

Christmas is a time for celebrating with family and friends and a time for traditions that make it special. In my family most of those traditions revolve around food. Christmas just doesn't seem like Christmas without a breakfast of plum dumplings and I couldn't imagine Christmas Eve without Russian Meat Pies. You might wonder how we ended up with a tradition of eating those tasty little meat pies on the night before Christmas when no one in my family has any Russian roots.

When I was a child my mother discovered the recipe in a newspaper she was reading and decided to try making them. They were delicious hot or cold. We enjoyed them so much that it became a special treat reserved for Christmas Eve. My Dad was working as a Hoist man in the mines back then and even though no one was working underground on the holiday he often had to work as a watchman on Christmas Eve. If he was working the 3 to 11 shift we would all get to stay up until he got home. We would have a cold supper at midnight of potato salad and Russian meat pies and celebrate the arrival of Christmas by opening our gifts before heading off to bed.

Once, he actually had to work from 11 till 7 the next morning and my mother decided to pack up a cooler with our midnight supper. Dad asked his boss if he could bring his family to work that night and once he got permission we all went to the mine together. Dad issued hard hats to Mom and my brother, Tom, and I, and we camped out in the

Eyes Wide Open

Hoist room with him for the whole night. When he went to do his rounds, Tom, and I went along with him.

We got to see the hoist that he normally operated and the change room where each miner's gear hung from the ceiling. We watched Dad "punch the clock" by inserting a card into a machine that would punch a hole in it showing the time he passed at each of the stops on his tour of inspection.

We drank tea from a thermos and ate our meat pies and potato salad pretending we were miners ourselves. Eventually we fell asleep on a bench while Mom and Dad passed the long hours of the night talking softly so as not to disturb us. It was the most memorable Christmas of all.

In my own family we have hot German Potato Salad and Russian meat pies for supper on Christmas Eve every year. It's an International meal that I look forward to with a lot of pleasure, mostly because of the memories it evokes. We don't eat the meat pies cold at midnight or out of a cooler the way we did when I was young but it still brings me back to those happy times in my childhood when the night before Christmas meant picnics with my Mom and Dad. Occasionally I sneak down to the refrigerator after the rest of the family is gone to bed just so I can have a cold one and remember.

Eyes Wide Open

Going Down

I've never been bold enough for gymnastics. Timidity works against you when it comes to tumbling routines. I did attempt an occasional headstand when I was a child but I never quite managed it. The only cartwheel I ever executed couldn't really be termed a success as it was entirely unintentional and I was wearing cross country skis at the time.

Cross country skiing is a popular winter activity in the Sudbury area. There are plenty of groomed trails to choose from. I had a friend in High School whose parents had come to Canada from Finland and she introduced me to the sport. Of course, she'd been skiing since she first learned to walk and she made it look effortless. I struggled along in her wake and every time I thought I was finally getting into the rhythm of it, my skis would cross and I'd end up tripping myself and falling. It was going to require some serious practice to be able to achieve the kind of grace she displayed.

I bought a pair of skis of my own when I was in College and I was anxious to try them out. Aino-Liisa had moved away by then but my friends, Karen and Don, were keen to join me on the trails. Of the three of us, Karen was the only one who was an experienced skier. Perhaps it had something to do with having Scandinavian roots. Her parents came to Canada from Denmark and she could ski as well as Aino-Liisa had. Don and I were the amateurs.

Eyes Wide Open

We were muddling along fairly well and gaining in confidence when we came to a trail marked "Intermediate".

"Should we try it?" I asked.

"Let's go for it," Don insisted. "We can do it."

We set off with Karen in the lead and for the most part we managed it just fine. We were about three fourths of the way through when we found ourselves at the top of quite a steep hill. Don and I waited there while Karen sped down the slope and stopped herself at the bottom.

"Lean forward a little," she called back to us. "Keep your legs together and your knees bent."

Never one to hesitate, Don launched himself and fairly flew down the trail. He nearly made it to the bottom but ended in a spectacular crash that left him almost completely buried in a snowdrift. He finally extricated himself and shook the snow out of his hair, digging around to find his missing hat.

"Watch out for the bump about halfway down," he shouted.

I stood poised on the brink for several seconds trying to work up my nerve with the two of them watching me from below. It was pride that finally pushed me over the edge. Once I was committed I did my best to follow Karen's advice. I kept my legs together with my knees bent. The wind in my face and the sense of speed was

Eyes Wide Open

incredible and exhilarating. Then I hit the bump Don warned me about. What he failed to mention was that I would find myself airborne at that point. It startled me so much that I unwittingly stood straight up, all instructions forgotten.

I completely lost my balance and I knew in an instant that I was going down. My bottom hit the ground first and I'm a little foggy on the details after that point. My modified cartwheel landed me at the bottom of the hill with all my limbs intact if somewhat tangled. With a little help I managed to ascertain that the only thing broken was one of my skis. The end had completely snapped off and it looked like I would be walking the rest of the way back to the road.

"Well…" I muttered, "That was fun."

I think Don would have liked to climb back up and try it again but we knew it would take a while to reach the end of the trail with me trudging through the snow carrying the pieces of my skis under an arm. We decided to forego any repeat performances and keep forging ahead. I couldn't bring myself to be upset about my broken ski when I was so thankful to be able to walk at all. I guess you could say I was never cut out for gymnastics or for racing down hill on a pair of skies, and especially not for a combination of the two.

Eyes Wide Open

Dare to Dream

I had a birthday recently. I am long past the days of candles on cakes but I am not above making a wish or two even now. These days we call them goals and add them to our bucket list. My mother was a great one for making wishes. All through my childhood we blew out candles and wrestled good-naturedly over wishbones whenever a turkey got roasted. We'd spend hours sitting in the middle of a clover patch looking for that elusive four-leafed specimen. My mother thought it would bring her luck but mostly we just enjoyed the hunt for something rare and the triumph that comes along with success. I suppose that's why I used to enjoy the "Where's Waldo" books that were popular years ago.

I remember sitting on the back porch on long summer afternoons and playing a game with my Mom that involved her imaginary "presto" machine. We would take turns sharing our fondest wishes and then we would presto them into existence. Of course one thing would lead to another until the dream we built grew to massive proportions bordering on the ridiculous. It was a happy game…almost on a par with the times we recorded ourselves giggling and laughing hysterically on a cassette player until we'd filled the whole tape. Then we would play it back and try to keep our faces straight as we listened. It's actually quite impossible to do.

We learned two important lessons from those games. Laughter really is good medicine and exercising

Eyes Wide Open

your imagination is a wonderful way to open up new worlds and explore outside the ordinary every day bonds of life. We learned that it was okay to dream and even to dream big. When you dream together with someone you both get a glimpse into each other's hearts.

My husband and I keep a list of dreams and wishes. Who knows? We may even achieve some of them. In the meantime, just talking about them gives me a sense that we have a lot to look forward to and I love that.

Thanks, Mom.

Eyes Wide Open

Driver Training

It's strange to think how far we've come in one generation although I suppose that every generation feels the same. My parents didn't grow up with cars. My mother's first experience behind the wheel of a vehicle was almost her last. My Dad was away at his job for the Department of Highways back in the late 1940's and Mom was at home on the farm near Noelville in Northern Ontario.

They had hired a man to help with the hay while Dad was at work so she and the hired man were forking hay into the wagon when the unthinkable happened. Mom decided she needed a drink of water so she gave the pitchfork she'd been using a hard thrust to stand it upright in the hay that lay knee deep where they stood. The hired man straightened with a grunt and Mom glanced over, a question in her eyes.

"You stuck the fork through my foot," he announced in a calm voice that was at odds with the way his face drained of color.

"Oh, no!" she cried dropping to her knees to brush the hay aside. Sure enough, the fork had gone straight through the top of his foot to pin him neatly to the earth. She lifted tear filled eyes to stare at him and tried to think through her panic. It was a disaster and it was her fault.

Eyes Wide Open

"You'd better pull it out," he instructed through gritted teeth. "…One quick pull."

She took a deep breath and pulled the fork free, tossing it aside before helping him to the front seat of the truck he'd arrived in. They managed to get his boot off and staunch the bleeding with a couple of handkerchiefs but she knew she had to get him to the doctor and there was only one way to do it. She never could remember how she managed to get the truck started and into first gear or how she was able to keep it on the road and pointed in the right direction on that drive into Noelville. It was only later, sitting in the parking lot at the hospital that reaction set in. The hired man had been admitted and she sat behind the wheel of the truck in a state of near paralysis. A policeman happened by and stopped to ask what the problem was.

"I can't get home," she responded in a forlorn voice. "I don't know how to drive."

It was at least fifteen years before Mom worked up the nerve to try driving once again. We owned a black Volkswagen Beetle and my oldest brother, Richard, decided he would teach her. My Dad was only too glad to let him. He could guess at just how stressful that undertaking would be and he wisely chose to stay out of it. Mom couldn't seem to get behind the wheel without falling into a state of near panic. It was a tribute to her force of will and Richard's determination that they persevered.

The first time Mom drove on the highway she got a ticket for driving too slowly and holding up traffic. In the

Eyes Wide Open

end she couldn't pass her road test because she got so flustered when she attempted to parallel park that she ended up backing over the curb and up onto the sidewalk. No matter how hard she tried to correct the problem she wound up back on the sidewalk each time. Much to her disgust, her second road test also failed and for the same reason. She refused to give up though. She practiced relentlessly and it was on her third try that she finally succeeded and came home a fully licensed driver. It gave her a measure of independence that she treasured.

Of course, that didn't mean she was a great driver. She never fully relaxed in a car. Even when my parents went from a standard to an automatic she still used both feet to drive. She always gripped the steering wheel with her two hands, knuckles white with tension. She would sit leaning forward with her chin thrust out and her shoulders hunched, a look of intense concentration pinching her face. It didn't inspire confidence in those of us who were passengers. I always imagined that was exactly how she must have looked on that long ago day when she drove the truck all the way to Noelville to get the hired man to the help he needed. Back then the hired man had problems of his own and probably didn't notice.

I have to admit that in spite of her anxieties or maybe because of them, she never had an accident in all her years of driving. She may have looked awkward and even a little frightening in the driver's seat but she managed to stay safe all the same. I reminded myself of that the year I turned 16 and she volunteered to teach me.

Eyes Wide Open

All the Conveniences

My brothers, Richard and Dave, along with a friend of theirs named Al pooled their resources back in the 70's and bought a 50 acre lot on St. Joseph's Island near Sault Ste. Marie in Ontario. They hoped to eventually clear a spot in the woods and build a log cabin for themselves. Of course it would be quite a while before that dream could become a reality and they would need a place to live in the meantime. The area was quite isolated but there was an old abandoned farmhouse nearby that looked like it might do in a pinch. Dave and Al decided to locate the owner and ask if they might fix it up a bit and stay in it over the winter. Richard would join them the following summer.

It wasn't much of a house. It hadn't been lived in for about twenty years and the glass had been broken out of all the windows. The inside was littered with the accumulated detritus of years of exposure to the elements. There was only one room on the main floor and it was about 15 feet square. A lean-to on the back of the house made a handy place to store firewood. There was a loft reached by a set of rickety stairs and the floor seemed solid enough even though the walls let in the light in a few places. There was no electricity or plumbing at all so it would mean living rough. Undeterred, the boys eventually found the elderly couple who owned the place and discovered that they had no objections to having it occupied once again if it could be made live-able.

Eyes Wide Open

It didn't take long to replace the missing glass in the windows and clean out the trash. There was an old wood stove made of sheet metal that would provide their only heat. It looked like a giant oval stove pipe with a hinged lid on the top. Dave christened it Tin Lizzie on the first day they lit a fire in it. That stove was going to keep them alive for the winter. It gave off plenty of warmth but it went through fuel at an alarming rate. With a little judicious patching of the walls here and there they could keep the worst of the drafts out but they were going to have to cut and haul a lot of wood to keep old Lizzie burning.

They had three coal oil lamps and a good supply of candles for light. Their cooking would have to be done on a camp stove and there was a root cellar where they could store their food. Water was going to be the real problem. They built a sled that would hold two large garbage cans and every few days they would drag it about a half mile to the creek to fill those cans with water. There would be no baths till spring. A covered bucket had to serve as a toilet since the only alternative was to go out and squat in the snow.

I'm sure it felt like the longest winter in history. By the time spring arrived and the snow melted both Dave and Al were more than ready for a little break from each other's company. Al moved into an old trailer that he fixed up and Richard took his place in the farmhouse with Dave. The first order of business that summer was to dig a well near the house. What unbelievable luxury it was to have a source of water just a few short steps from the door! They found a discarded bathtub that eventually came to occupy a place of honor right next to the well in the yard. The ease of filling it in its new location took precedence over any need for privacy.

Once the water question was dealt with they decided to go all out and build an outhouse. My Dad and my younger brother, Tom, showed up to help. They chose a spot some distance from the house and started to dig. Once the hole was deep enough they went to work on cobbling together a shelter from bits and pieces of lumber they had collected. They even managed to find and install a toilet seat…the ultimate in outhouse comfort. They ended up building the whole thing so that it faced the bush rather than the house.

"That way we don't need to bother with a door," Richard announced with a grin. "It's better for ventilation."

"I never dreamed I'd think of an outhouse as a luxury but this is going to be great," Dave added.

They turned that old farmhouse into a home and ended up spending another entire winter in it before they were through. It gave them a taste of what it must have been like for my parents growing up…back in the days when having a well built outhouse made you the envy of the neighborhood.

Eyes Wide Open

Toothless

It's almost the end of the month and I happened to flip the page on my calendar to take a sneak peak at what to expect in the coming weeks. The first thing to catch my eye was a bright flag marking the occasion of my next dentist appointment. How could nine months have flown by so quickly? The gap between regular visits never seems long enough in my mind. I know I shouldn't complain. It's because of those regular visits that I still have all my own teeth and they remain relatively problem free. I didn't have that luxury when I was a child. Back in those days we only went to the dentist when we had a toothache that became unbearable. In all the years I was growing up I only ever sat in a dentist's chair twice and both times it was to have a tooth pulled.

My Dad used to tell stories of how one of his brothers pulled out his own teeth with a pair of pliers whenever they became too troublesome. There eventually came a day when he only had one or two teeth left and his smile had a decidedly forlorn quality to it. His one remaining front tooth stood all alone in the gap and I couldn't help but be reminded of the strange smiles we'd see carved into pumpkins every Halloween. At least no one could accuse him of vanity. I often wondered why he didn't just pull out that last tooth and get himself fitted with a set of dentures but perhaps he held on to it for sentimental reasons. As far as I know he never went to a dentist in his life.

Eyes Wide Open

My own parents each had a set of false teeth before they reached middle age. My mother used to take hers out and make faces at us when we were children. It made her look positively sinister and never failed to leave us shrieking in horrified glee as we scrambled to escape her clutching fingers and smacking lips. Then she would slip her teeth back into her mouth and simply be Mom again, blithely ignoring our giggling pleas for her to do it again. She liked to save that game for when we were least expecting it.

She and Dad were visiting us when our own children were little and Mom decided to try it out on the boys. They were sitting on her lap when she reached up and slipped her dentures into the palm of her hand and turned to grin at them, her cheeks sunken and her empty mouth stretched wide. Their initial reaction was all she could have wished for but curiosity quickly overcame any fear. Instead of trying to run away, Daniel crowded closer to get a better view and Jason took his cue from his older brother. They were clearly fascinated and wanted to know how she'd done it. She had to put her teeth in and take them out several more times before they were satisfied.

A couple of days later I found Daniel rummaging around in the kitchen drawer where we kept a few household tools. He came up with the hammer we used for hanging pictures and he definitely looked like a boy with a mission in mind.

"What do you need a hammer for?" I asked as I deftly plucked it out of his hand.

Eyes Wide Open

"My teeth are stuck," he complained. "I can't get them out."

I just stood there in stunned surprise. Clearly I was going to have to do some debriefing after my Mom's little game. It was one of those occasions where I just happened to be in the right place at the right time. I shudder to think what might have happened if Daniel had been able to carry through with his intent before I had a chance to explain the difference between false teeth and real. He might have ended up with a smile like my uncle's.

Eyes Wide Open

Shivareed

I'd never heard of a Shivaree until I met my husband, Bev. It was a custom in the rural communities he grew up in that involved family and friends of a newlywed couple staging a nocturnal visit to the hapless bride and groom as soon as they'd set up house together. The crowd would show up at the door with every sort of noise maker imaginable and set up a clamor that would rouse even the soundest sleeper. They wouldn't quit until their rudely awakened victims struggled into robes and slippers and opened the door to invite them all in for a cup of tea.

Over the years the practice evolved to include the playing of pranks. Bev recounted stories of how he and his family and friends would find a way to sneak into the home of the couple they intended to Shivaree and do all sorts of mischief. They would strip the labels off of the cans in the kitchen cupboard or stitch the cuffs together on a shirt or two hanging in the closet.

In one unforgettable instance they plugged in all the appliances they could find and left them turned on while they flipped the main breaker off. As soon as the young couple returned home and realized they had no power they switched the breaker back on, and the resulting din combined with shouts of "surprise" from all the culprits hidden in closets was enough to frighten them out of a year's growth. Things just kept getting more and more out of hand as the young people got more creative.

Eyes Wide Open

    I started hearing the stories as the date of our own wedding drew near and I was frankly horrified. One friend recounted how they had emerged from the church on their wedding day to find that their car had been set on blocks and all four wheels removed. We also heard stories of brides being kidnapped by the so-called friends of the groom before the reception could get underway. I became very vocal about how I was likely to react should anyone be foolish enough to attempt such a thing with us.

    Bev had to confess that after some of the Shivarees he'd been a part of we were going to have to expect some attempt at payback. He spent a good deal of thought and effort in the days leading up to our wedding to prevent that very thing. He actually nailed our windows shut and let it be known that we had neighbors with instructions to keep an eye on our house in our absence. He thought there might be a possibility that we would be followed to the location we'd chosen for our wedding night so all plans were made in the utmost secrecy.

    We packed our suitcases and stowed them in our car which he then hid in some obscure parking lot in the city. He arranged with his brother that we would leave the reception hidden in the back seat of his car and then be dropped off a block or two from where our own car was parked. Once Bev could be certain we were not followed we could walk the rest of the way to retrieve our vehicle and set out in earnest.

    Unfortunately, in all his elaborate precautions, he failed to take into account that his parents and younger

Eyes Wide Open

sisters would be spending a night in our house before they set out for home. We returned from our week long honeymoon to discover that we had not escaped unscathed after all.

Every tea towel we owned had been knotted together into one long rope and the entryway was festooned with ribbons and bows. A gallon or two of confetti had been stashed in various places throughout the house like heat vents and teacups. We had a glass canister filled with popcorn that we found liberally laced with confetti and over the next few days we kept discovering it in the most unlikely locations like the toes of whatever socks we'd left in the dresser.

Bev eventually discovered his work clothes hidden between the mattress and box spring on our bed after he realized they were missing from the closet. It was months later when I accidentally bumped a picture hanging on the wall as I was vacuuming the floor and was unexpectedly showered with confetti that had been carefully stashed behind it. I laughed so hard it hurt.

I suppose you could say we got Shivareed *in absentia*. I think we got off lightly considering some of the tricks Bev had been guilty of in his youth. It ended up being a lot of harmless fun and I know he would have been disappointed if no one had bothered to try anything.

That next summer I was attempting to open a window in our bedroom and found it to be stuck. I struggled with it for a good twenty minutes before I

Eyes Wide Open

remembered that they'd all been nailed shut the previous year in Bev's attempt to outfox the pranksters in the family. He ended up sealing the house with the pranksters inside.

"Maybe we actually Shivareed ourselves!"

Eyes Wide Open

Frog Legs

When my Dad was growing up in the woods of Northern Ontario he learned a great deal about those things that were edible in his environment and those that were not. Much of that knowledge was passed down to him from his parents although he did confess that whenever my Grandma Landry pointed out something that was poisonous and warned him away from it when he was a boy, he usually ended up taking a bite of it as soon as her back was turned. He was always careful not to swallow but his curiosity demanded that he see for himself what it tasted like.

Once my younger brother, Tom, and I were old enough to tag along on hikes through the woods with Dad, he would point out the things he'd learned as a boy. We tried what he called winterberries and thought they tasted a little like minty toothpaste. We learned to recognize and enjoy eating the leaves of a plant he named sour grass. He declared that he and his brothers and sisters had grown up chewing spruce gum instead of the gumballs we were so fond of so we tried that as well. I can't say it tempted me to make a habit of it. It was chewy all right but it tasted like medicine of the most unpleasant sort.

Our favorite part of any day in the woods with my Dad was when we stopped for lunch. After our experimental nibbles on the plants Dad showed us, the food we'd brought from home looked awfully tempting. He would set us to gathering sticks to make a fire so he could put water on to boil. He had an old tomato juice can rigged

Eyes Wide Open

with a wire handle that he could set on a stone near the flames with a couple of tea bags tossed in. It was perfect for making bush tea if you didn't mind a few bits of ash floating in the brew. He would cut and sharpen some sticks so we could toast our bologna sandwiches and nothing ever tasted better.

We were looking forward to our usual lunch on one of our many fishing trips with Dad so when the sun stood directly overhead we began looking for a good spot to pull the canoe out of the water. The lake we were on was a small one and the spot we chose had a rocky point where we could cast in our lines and fish from the shore for a while before we headed back out. We were just getting ready to start the fire when one of us asked Dad if he'd ever tasted frog legs.

"Sure," he replied with a shrug. "They taste like chicken."

Tom and I looked at each other and it was plain that our thoughts were racing along in tandem.

I leaned a little closer. "How did you cook them…the frogs?"

"You find me a nice big bullfrog and I'll show you."

"Can we take the canoe?" Tom asked.

Dad waved his hand in the general direction of the lake and we jumped to our feet and scrambled to launch the

Eyes Wide Open

boat. There was a little bay choked with cattails and tall grass that looked like a perfect haven for frogs and we lost no time heading in that direction.

There was an old saying that helped when it came to identifying a frog by the sound it made. Small frogs could be heard to pipe out with a shrill "Too deep! Too deep!" where a bullfrog would croak out with a deep bass "Go round! Go round!" That "Go round!" was what we were listening for as we eased the canoe through the lily pads and reeds close to shore.

We did find the bullfrog we wanted but grabbing it without tipping ourselves into the water was next to impossible. We just couldn't get near enough. It took several attempts at a stealthy approach before Tom, losing patience, suddenly swung his paddle in a whistling overhead arc, giving the frog a whack on the head that was surely lethal. It left him floating belly up and within our reach at last. It was a simple matter to retrieve our prize and head back across the lake to where Dad was waiting.

We were nearly there when Tom shouted a warning and I twisted around to see that the corpse in the bottom of the canoe was starting to twitch and then struggling to right itself. For a few moments chaos reigned while we tried to reach the frog without capsizing the boat.

Bullfrogs are slippery and this one was particularly frantic. Perhaps he had an inkling of our murderous intent because he put the very legs that we'd been hoping to taste

Eyes Wide Open

to excellent use and leaped right out of the canoe to disappear in the waters below.

We never did get to taste frog legs on that day or any other. It was back to bologna sandwiches for us.

Eyes Wide Open

On the Roof

I've never been able to adopt a cavalier attitude when it comes to heights. Ladders have always been a challenge to me. Back when I was in College my family lived in a small one and a half story house. I came home one day to find the doors all locked and myself without a key. I remembered my father mentioning that you could get in through the upstairs window which was accessible from the porch roof. I stood there weighing my options and finally decided that the porch roof wasn't really all that high. I was reasonably certain that I could manage to get up there and climb through the window. Besides, the prospect of standing around in the yard until someone came home didn't hold much appeal.

I fetched the ladder from the shed and carefully leaned it up against the eaves trough. I was halfway up when I realized I probably should have set the base of it a little further from the wall. It didn't feel at all secure but I told myself it was likely my nerves that were making everything wobble. I gritted my teeth and kept moving upward one agonizing rung at a time. When I managed to crawl onto the roof it was with considerable pride in the accomplishment. Then I attempted to get the window open and discovered that it wouldn't budge.

I struggled with it for a good ten minutes before I gave it one final frustrated thump and ungraciously conceded defeat. I made my way back to the ladder but one look at the ground below convinced me that there was no

Eyes Wide Open

way on earth I could bring myself to step out onto that precarious perch. I was going to have to wait it out after all. How humiliating! I spent the next two hours pretending that I'd climbed up there deliberately to get a suntan and do some cloud watching. I determined that from then on I would leave the roof to the birds and squirrels and keep my own feet on the ground. I wasn't counting on eventually having a son like Jason.

He was only in Grade 1 when he climbed the tree beside our house. When he got near the top the tree bent over just enough to allow him to jump onto the roof of our porch. Unfortunately, as soon as he let go it sprang back into its former position which was quite out of reach. He was trapped on that porch roof just as I had been on that long ago day when I failed miserably at my one and only attempt at breaking and entering.

When his brother, Daniel, came to tell me what happened I had to fight to disguise my rising anxiety. There was no one else to do what had to be done. The only ladder I could find was a step ladder that was nowhere near tall enough. I pasted a smile on my face and climbed up to the top step. I was going to have to let go and reach up with both hands to where Jason sat waiting for me to rescue him. It just didn't bear thinking about. It's amazing what you can accomplish when one of your children needs you. I even managed to appear reasonably calm and matter of fact in a performance that should have won me an Oscar. At least Jason came out of the whole experience with no emotional baggage.

Eyes Wide Open

Eventually he got a job as a roofer to pay for his College education and I did my best to be supportive. Unlike me, he was completely at home on rooftops. He liked to entertain us at the dinner table by recounting some of his more hair-raising experiences on the job. Those stories convinced me that it was probably best that I couldn't actually watch him at work. Hearing about a slide down a steep pitch when you're sitting safe in your own home is much easier than watching it happen.

"Don't worry Mom," Jason reassured me. "We're wearing a rope."

I tried to imagine it. "What do you tie the rope to?" I asked.

He never batted an eye. "We tie off to each other and then work on opposite sides of the roof."

I froze, my fork poised halfway to my open mouth.

"That way if one of us slips over the edge, the other can jump off the roof on his side to keep us both from hitting the ground."

There was a split second of silence before the snickers started and I realized I'd been had. I shook my head and bounced a dinner roll off of Jason's chest to wipe the grin off his face. Roofers have their own twisted sense of humor. I decided it was better not to ask questions. Instead I just made it my business to pray for him every day. Birds, squirrels...and Jason.

Eyes Wide Open

Hitting the Jackpot

I love learning where various unusual words or expressions originated. When I was growing up we often heard people use the phrase "What a jackpot!" to describe a place or situation that was a total mess. More often, though, when you heard the word jackpot you thought of an unexpected windfall of either money or other good fortune. The term actually comes from the early 1900s and the game of poker in which you need at least a pair of jacks or higher in order to open a hand. The pot is the total amount of money wagered and the winner gets the jackpot. Because a number of hands are often dealt before anyone can open and players must put in money for each round, the jackpot tends to be quite large.

My mother never played poker but she did play Bingo whenever she got an opportunity. The largest prize of the night was called the jackpot and it was played for in the last game of the evening which was a blackout game. That meant that every one of the numbers on your card had to be covered in order for you to win. The game would continue until someone finally called "Bingo" to indicate they had a winning card. If there was more than one winner, the prize was shared.

My brother, Richard, remembers a night before I was born back in the mid fifties when Dad was working the late shift at the mine and Mom was having her night out at the Bingo. She arrived home at the end of the evening and

Eyes Wide Open

the boys knew immediately that something momentous must have occurred. She burst through the door of our mobile home clutching her purse to her chest, her eyes wide and her whole face lit with excitement.

"Come and see!" she chortled as she danced her way down the narrow hallway to the back bedroom. She opened her purse and began pulling out handfuls of cash to toss onto the bed while Richard and Dave stood gaping at the spectacle. It certainly looked like an enormous pile of money.

"I won the jackpot! $350 and I was the only winner!"

Mom began meticulously laying out the bills side by side on the bed just so she could see all of them at once. The prize had been paid out in small denominations so by the time she was through arranging it all, her winnings covered the entire mattress in a bizarre parody of a paper bedspread.

"I think I'll just leave it all right where it is," she announced. She couldn't stop smiling. She was practically rubbing her hands together in gleeful anticipation of the look on Dad's face when he came home.

The boys got hustled off to their bunks but sleep was impossible. When my mother was excited about something the whole household was electrified. The hands on the clock moved with glacial slowness as they awaited Dad's arrival at the end of his shift. When he finally did

Eyes Wide Open

walk through the door he was a little surprised to find Mom waiting up for him. She took his lunch box and thermos from him and set them on the counter quickly to disguise the fact that her hands were shaking. She hardly dared look at him for fear of giving herself away. Dad was busy hanging his coat in the closet and didn't notice anything amiss. He headed for the bedroom and Richard and Dave held their collective breath, pretending to be asleep as he passed by the door they'd left ajar in their eagerness not to miss anything. Mom trailed closely behind him.

He reached for the light switch as he entered the room they shared and then froze at the strange spectacle that confronted him when the darkness fled. "What the....!?" He turned quickly to see Mom, her face wreathed in smiles, doing her own unique version of the Happy Dance behind him while muffled giggles sounded from the darkened room he'd just passed. As surprises went, it was a huge success. Mom had hit the jackpot in more ways than one.

Eyes Wide Open

Unwanted Guests

We finally installed our second garage door opener this past Christmas and what a luxury it is not to have to get out of the car to open or close the door manually every time we go out. We did it the old fashioned way for years and I admit that there were times when we just left it open to save ourselves the inconvenience. That was before we discovered that the open door was a tempting invitation to the local wildlife to come in out of the cold.

We'd had an occasional bird find its way in but that wasn't entirely unexpected. I was considerably more unnerved the morning I stepped through the connecting door into the garage to be confronted with evidence that something much larger than a bird had been inadvertently locked in overnight. There were muddy tracks all over the hood of our car and my husband, Bev's workbench was adorned with a pile of droppings that had certainly not come from any bird.

A closer examination of the paw prints on the car confirmed that our intruder was undoubtedly a raccoon. I took a quick look around, half expecting the beast to jump out at me from some darkened corner. I didn't see anything but that didn't prevent me from scurrying back into the house where I reported my findings to Bev and left the whole thing in his capable hands.

An hour later he came in still armed with a flashlight to announce that it was indeed a raccoon and that he'd

Eyes Wide Open

discovered its hiding place. Apparently there was a small opening near the rafters in the garage that led to a narrow space between the roof and the ceiling of the adjoining front porch. The coon was making itself at home in the farthest corner of that space and Bev said it looked to be the size of a small Volkswagen in the feeble glow of his light. He went out to the porch and stood gazing speculatively at the ceiling for a few moments.

"It's probably going to want to stay right there till dark," he mused. "I just don't want it to decide to take up permanent residence."

He opened the garage door to provide an escape route and then proceeded to try to drive our unwanted guest out of its secure bolt hole. He put a thick padded glove on the end of a broom handle and used it to pound relentlessly on the ceiling at the point where he judged the raccoon to be resting. There was some slight scuffling but none of it was moving in the direction of freedom. When it was obvious that a new tactic was needed, Bev abandoned the broom and went to fetch a portable radio. He set it up directly below the spot where the coon lay and tuned it to the most abrasive music he could find before cranking the volume up to an unbearable level.

"At least it won't get the idea that this is a good place to sleep," Bev announced, his smile grim.

I nodded mutely and went to look for earplugs. In the meantime, Bev went back out to the garage to rig up a makeshift trap. He took an extra large plastic garbage can

Eyes Wide Open

and secured it to the edge of the workbench so it couldn't be tipped over. It was deep and the sides were smooth and offered no purchase for climbing. He placed an open can of sardines in the bottom of the can thinking that the raccoon wouldn't be able to resist the odorous treat and would end up jumping down after it only to discover it impossible to climb out again. He positioned a few empty soup cans on the workbench so that he would hear the raccoon's approach and then retreated into the house to wait.

It was late in the day when we heard the rattle and crash of a soup can rolling to the concrete floor and knew that our hungry visitor had been lured from its hiding place to investigate the tantalizing scent of sardines that had been wafting around the garage all day. Apparently raccoons are not as stupid as we'd hoped. Not even sardines could tempt it into that garbage can once it learned that the can wouldn't tip over. By the time Bev got out there the coon was gone.

"Waste of a perfectly good can of sardines," he muttered as he inspected the scattered soup cans and the empty trap.

He was able to find fresh tracks leading outside and he wasted no time in locking everything up so that there would be no returning. The hole leading to the space above the porch ceiling got sealed up that very night and the next day he borrowed a proper live trap to set up just outside the garage. The raccoon was eventually caught trying to find a way back inside and we were able to get rid of it at last.

Eyes Wide Open

That whole experience made it clear that leaving the garage door open for the sake of convenience was a choice with consequences. I probably owe that raccoon a debt of gratitude. That was the day the idea to invest in a garage door opener was born.

Eyes Wide Open

Reluctant Soldier

My Grandpa Landry spent a short time in the army when he was drafted in May of 1918. He never did end up going overseas to fight because the war ended a few months later. He received his discharge and he and my grandmother settled back into life on a farm in the Noelville area and began to raise a family. He hoped that his own sons would never be faced with the prospect of fighting a war but that hope was in vain.

My Dad travelled to Toronto in March of 1945 to enlist in the Canadian Infantry Corps during the final months of World War II. He had no way of knowing that the war would end that very year. He was 20 years old.

He was sent to Quebec for basic training and his stories of life on the base there left us all with the impression that he hated every minute of it. He never felt that he fit in with the rest of the men. Being raised in Ontario meant that he spoke French with an accent that set him apart and he was nearly a head taller than every other man there. The rest of the recruits thought of him as some sort of country bumpkin and he got into a number of fights before they learned to leave him strictly alone.

Not all of the fights had to do with him and his difficulty fitting in. His roommate was probably one of the shortest men there and the two of them looked like a very oddly matched pair when they went into town together. Having my Dad at his side gave the fellow a boldness he

Eyes Wide Open

never would have shown otherwise and that meant trouble. I suppose he figured no one would mess with him as long as there was a chance my Dad would step in to back him up. They were in a bar one night and Dad was minding his own business but his roommate was a little drunk and got pretty mouthy with a couple of other soldiers. They eyed Dad warily and left without making a fuss. Eventually, his roommate decided to head back to the barracks even though my Dad wasn't ready to leave yet. He set out on his own and that turned out to be a big mistake.

One of the men he had insulted earlier was waiting for him there and when my Dad finally arrived it was to find his roommate severely beaten and in the process of being throttled by a very determined attacker. It looked like murder was being done and Dad jumped in without even thinking about it. The fight was over quickly with his roommate's assailant ending up in the hospital with a broken jaw and Dad wishing for a different roommate. He wasn't expecting to have to fight his way through the whole regiment before ever facing the enemy.

Dad's one great fear was that his superiors would find out that he was a crack shot with a rifle and decide to make him into a sniper. He could handle the idea of a face to face fight but he couldn't bear the thought of being asked to shoot a man from hiding. He just didn't think he could do it. He had been hunting since childhood but he decided he'd better keep that bit of information to himself. He pretended to be clumsy in cleaning and handling his gun in the hopes that his awkwardness would convince his officers that he had little experience with firearms. He took special

Eyes Wide Open

care to miss when it came to target practice even though it would have been a simple matter to hit the mark every time.

Putting on such an act was a strain for a man who hated dishonesty as much as my Dad did, but he felt he had no choice. News that the war was over came as a welcome relief.

He wanted desperately to be transferred back to Ontario and even dreamed of just walking away and disappearing into the forest one day. He knew that if he chose to do it they would never find him. His sense of duty won out in the end. He remained where he was until the order for his transfer was issued at last and he returned to Ontario thinking of home. He was discharged to return to civilian life when the army was demobilized in May of 1946, just before his 22nd birthday.

He'd been a soldier for 14 months and even though he never saw a battlefield the experience left him absolutely convinced that he wasn't cut out for army life. He could hardly wait to get back to the farm.

Eyes Wide Open

I Think I Can

My Dad was a great believer in willpower. He always insisted that once he decided he was going to do something there was nothing on earth that could stop him. In the course of a lifetime I've learned not to underestimate the importance of that kind of steely determination. It can mean the difference between success and failure when the odds are stacked against you.

I suppose I may have inherited a tiny bit of my Dad's stubborn will. At least it shows up occasionally when I tackle jobs that are manifestly too big for me. That was the case when I decided to move some furniture to an upstairs bedroom in our farmhouse. I managed to tip the dressers, minus their drawers, onto their polished tops and so was able to slide them along on the wall to wall carpet without much difficulty. Even the stairs which were also carpeted posed no great obstacle as I pushed each piece up to the second floor.

I kept at it until only the wardrobe was left to move. It stood at least a foot taller than I was and looked massive. It did occur to me that I was being a tad foolish but I was determined to finish the job. I'd just have to be smart about it. I wrestled the wardrobe to the foot of the stairs moving first one side and then the other a few inches at a time. Once there I very carefully tipped it onto its side so that it rested against the stairs. I got my shoulder under the bottom of it and somehow managed to straighten my legs and start it moving.

Eyes Wide Open

It was even heavier than I'd imagined but by then I was committed. I couldn't figure out how to extricate myself so I struggled onward with every muscle vibrating with the strain. I was two thirds of the way up when I lost my balance for a moment and the force of gravity took over. I ended up slipping with the monstrous weight of the wardrobe bearing down on me and I lost several inches before I managed to stop my downward slide.

I froze, paralyzed by the vision of me lying crumpled at the bottom of the stairs, the wardrobe splintered to kindling on top of me. If ever there was a need for a healthy dose of my Dad's willpower it was in that moment. I tapped into reserves I didn't know I had and resumed my slow upward progress. I managed it in the end but you can bet that my husband, Bev, had words for me when he got home and discovered what I'd done. What was I thinking indeed?

They say that the acorn doesn't fall far from the tree and I must say that my daughter, Lauren, has also been known to tackle obstacles with that same disregard for what other people might see as her limitations. She's never been very big and some might even think her fragile. They would be mistaken in that. What she lacks in muscle she makes up for in the strength of her will and her indomitable spirit.

Back when she was thirteen or so she and Bev went on a father and daughter canoe trip with another Dad who had twin girls. The trip involved a 300 meter portage and Lauren was determined to pull her weight when they

Eyes Wide Open

reached that point. The men shouldered the canoes and moved off along the trail leaving the girls with the packs. They planned to come back for anything the girls couldn't carry.

That probably should have included the pack that Lauren decided to take. It looked as though it weighed more than she did and that might not have been a stretch. She wore size 0 in those days. It wasn't easy but she somehow managed to get it hoisted onto her back and once she settled her shoulders into the harness and got her balance she lost no time in marching off after the others who'd gone ahead.

The trail was a bit rough in places. There was even a low section built up with logs like an old corduroy road. That was where she came to grief. One slip and her feet shot out from under her landing her squarely on her back. Luckily the pack broke her fall. Then again, maybe it wasn't so lucky. Once she caught her breath she discovered that she couldn't get up with the heavy pack anchoring her to the earth. With her arms and legs in the air she felt much like a turtle that has been flipped onto its back. No matter how hard she struggled she just couldn't get herself turned over.

She was just about to try extricating herself from the harness when another canoeist happened along and, seeing her dilemma, reached down to grab the top of the pack where it protruded above her head. With one heave he lifted the heavy pack with Lauren still strapped in and set her back on her feet. Undaunted, she offered him a slightly

Eyes Wide Open

red-faced thank you before resuming her trek. She managed the rest of the trail without incident and I have no doubt that given the chance, she might have tried carrying the canoe as well. I wasn't surprised at all when I heard the story. There's a little of my Dad in both of us.

Eyes Wide Open

Stand Up and Stand Out

     I once had a saleswoman try to help me pick out earrings that would fit with my personal style. I've never thought of myself as having a particular style but she was quick to disabuse me of that notion. Apparently everyone has a personal style whether they realize it or not. There are those whose style is "classic" while others could be labeled "flamboyant". Some might be termed "dramatic" and some simply "eclectic". It didn't take her long to come to the conclusion that my style was what she termed as "natural". Perhaps the fact that I rarely bother to wear make-up was a dead give-away. In any case, she was probably right in her assessment. No one would ever liken me to a bird of paradise. I like to keep things simple and my preference has always been to avoid a lot of attention....no wild and crazy hairstyles, chunky jewelry, or multi-colored nails for me.

     My aversion to standing out in a crowd stems back to my early teens and those years when I first began to be conscious of what other people thought of me. Some people might glory in being different from the majority of their peers but I wasn't one of them. I just wanted to blend in. There is something to be said for the advocates of school uniforms. We didn't have uniforms in my High School but there was a dress code back when I started into Grade 9. Pants were not allowed except on rare designated "Wear What You Want Days".

Eyes Wide Open

Eventually, the intrepid members of our student counsel lobbied successfully to have the outdated dress code rescinded and every day became a Wear What You Want Day.

Of course in order to wear what I wanted I had to get it past my parents and that was a problem of a different sort. My parents had very definite opinions about clothes. They wanted me to wear a dress to the very first High School dance I ever attended. It took me forever to convince them that if I did I would most certainly be the only girl there wearing one. Jeans, the garment of choice for the youth of that day, were totally out of the question. As far as my parents were concerned, jeans were what you wore to work in the garden. They absolutely believed that I would be laughed at if I showed up at the dance wearing jeans.

My mother went out and bought me a brand new outfit….a white blouse with ruffles at the collar and cuffs and a pair of corduroy pants in a lovely gold color. Horrors! I wanted to go badly enough that I actually wore the outfit and prayed no one would really notice it in the darkened gymnasium. I'm thankful to say that once my parents heard that everyone else had indeed been wearing jeans, they shook their heads in baffled incomprehension, conceded that I might have been right after all and agreed to let me make my own choices from that point on.

That didn't mean I would never again be the focus of all eyes. Sometimes stuff just happens. We still wore dresses or skirts to school from time to time. I was wearing

Eyes Wide Open

a navy blue skirt on the day I was asked to come up to the front of the room to write on the blackboard during French class. As soon as I stood up and began to make my way forward I noticed a few muffled giggles behind me. I immediately checked to make sure that my slip hadn't somehow migrated downward to dangle below my hemline. It was a wardrobe malfunction not unheard of in those days.

Everything seemed in order so I proceeded to the front and began the task assigned to me. It wasn't easy because what had begun as one or two giggles was fast escalating to become the chuckles and snorts of an entire roomful of people trying desperately to restrain their laughter. I was mortified. I couldn't imagine what on earth they were laughing at. I scrambled to finish the sentence I was supposed to write so that I could hurry back to the comparative safety of my desk, my chin up and my entire face burning with embarrassment. My friend, Annie, who was seated in the desk directly behind mine was laughing so hard there were tears leaking from the corners of her eyes.

"What's so funny?" I demanded in a furious undertone.

She leaned forward to whisper haltingly in my ear. Apparently she had been resting her foot against the back of my chair earlier. There was a space between the chair back and the seat…just enough that when I rose to walk to the front of the class my navy blue skirt was no longer plain and simple. It was adorned with a perfect and very distinct footprint positioned exactly in the middle of my butt. I couldn't have stood out more if I'd tried.

Eyes Wide Open

Lost and Found

There is no worse feeling in the world than that which overtakes you when you lose track, even temporarily, of one of your children. I didn't really understand my mother's near hysterical reaction the year I was in kindergarten and I took my younger brother, Tom, to school with me one afternoon so that he could play on the swings in the yard. She didn't notice him leaving the house with me and it never once occurred to me that I should mention my idea to her before setting out. It seemed like such a good idea…at least until we got home.

Once I had children of my own I had opportunity to discover first-hand what that reaction was all about. We always wanted our children to grow into strong, independent adults with a keen sense of adventure and a desire to see what might lie around the next corner. We just didn't anticipate that the seeds of those very qualities would begin bearing fruit at such an early age.

Daniel was not quite three years old when I left him playing in the sandbox in our yard while I brought his baby brother into the house to place him in his crib for a nap. We lived on a farm and the house was set quite a distance from the road so I thought him safe enough for the few minutes I would be gone. I was wrong. When I returned his trucks lay abandoned in the sand and there was no sign of him.

I searched everywhere I could think of, getting more frantic by the minute until the only place I hadn't looked

Eyes Wide Open

was out at the highway. I broke into a stumbling run, my pulse pounding loud in my ears and my voice cracking as I shouted his name. The ditch stretched empty in both directions and I didn't know what to do. I was having a melt down every bit as hysterical as my own mother's had been all those years ago. Just then a car pulled out of the driveway of the neighboring farm where my husband was working and cruised to a stop in front of me. The woman driving was a stranger to me but she could see what a state I was in and she rolled the window down to ask if I was looking for a little boy.

"He's at the barn next door," she explained. "He was looking for his Dad."

Daniel had walked all the way to the next farm along the ATV trail that my husband, Bev, used to go to work. He'd ridden along it with his Dad a few times and he knew exactly where he was going. Bev had been trying to reach me on the phone. Those moments when I didn't know what had become of my son were the most terrifying that I have ever endured.

Once I could breath normally again, I offered up a silent apology to my mother for what she'd endured that long ago afternoon when Tom had gone missing. Bev was very sympathetic. He knew I was upset but he didn't really know what I'd been feeling until a similar thing happened to him a few years later

Once again it was our first-born who disappeared. I was out for the evening and Bev was putting the younger

Eyes Wide Open

two children to bed. Daniel, as the eldest, was allowed to play for a few extra minutes but when Bev came back downstairs he couldn't find him. At first he wasn't too alarmed. He searched the house but there was no sign of him so he thought he must have gone back out to the yard. By the time he'd searched the yard and both barns he was beginning to feel frantic. He burst back into the silent kitchen thinking he might have come in while he was looking elsewhere. He hurried from room to room calling out Daniel's name but there was no response. He'd been searching for at least 20 minutes, the longest minutes he'd ever experienced. Where could he have gone?

He was getting desperate and was beginning to wonder if he should call the police when a muffled giggle brought him up short. Two strides brought Bev to the kitchen table which was pushed back against the wall to save space when it was not in use. He flipped up the tablecloth and bent to peer into the face of one little boy curled up on the seat of the chair on the opposite side of the table.

"What are you doing?" he demanded, his voice trembling with a mixture of frustration and relief. "Why didn't you answer me when I called?"

Daniel crawled out, his tentative smile filled with childish innocence. "I was playing hide and seek," he explained.

He'd managed to stay hidden the entire time that Bev searched and who knows how long it would have taken

Eyes Wide Open

to find him if he hadn't given himself away in the end. To be fair, no one had ever told him that you can't play hide and seek unless everyone actually knows you are playing. No doubt he didn't really understand what all the fuss was about. At least no harm was done. Daniel grew up into the strong and independent adult we hoped he would become and Bev and I….we managed to survive the journey.

Eyes Wide Open

There's No Fool like an April Fool

Last Friday was April Fools' Day, one of the highlights of the year in my mother's thinking. She would plot and scheme for days in her determination to catch us unawares and have us fall prey to one of her tricks. It was the one day in the year when, for a few hours, it was acceptable to lie through your teeth. You could tell any kind of whopper and the object was to do it so convincingly that the person you were targeting actually believed you until you shouted a triumphant "April Fools!"

In our house you had to succeed on the first attempt or concede defeat for that year. Once people were reminded of what day it was they were on their guard and it was very nearly impossible to trick them. My Dad considered the whole thing foolishness, which was the point of the exercise after all.

He never did try any tricks of his own but he would smile indulgently at my Mom's enthusiastic efforts. I can't count the number of times she persuaded us to run to the window to see whatever it was that was getting her so excited that she was practically jumping up and down. I have to admit that she was a pretty good actress when she set her mind to it.

I remember with considerable pride the first year that I managed a preemptive strike that caught her completely by surprise and won the day for me before she even had a chance to put her own plans into action.

Eyes Wide Open

Sometimes the simplest idea works best and that morning I was inspired.

Mom was busy out in the kitchen when I woke up and headed to the bathroom. I took a few moments to compose myself in front of the mirror. I had to make sure that I could produce a look of consternation that would be utterly convincing. It wouldn't do to let a grin slip out to spoil the effect. When I was as ready as I could ever be I flushed the toilet. I gave it a few seconds before letting out a desperate shriek and bursting out the door.

"Mom," I shouted. "The toilet's overflowing!"

She didn't stop to ask questions. She flung open the door of the broom closet, took hold of the mop and rushed past me down the hall and into the bathroom to stem the flood she expected to find spreading over the linoleum. There was a moment of silence before she turned and came back out to face the music. My brother, Tom, and I were falling over ourselves laughing out in the hall.

"April Fools!" I gasped. "I got you! Finally, I got you!" It was a sweet victory.

Years later Bev and I happened to be visiting my parents on April 1st. We'd only been married a short while and Bev was still doing his best to make a good impression when we sat down to breakfast. I suppose it was my fault for not warning him. Halfway through the meal my mother looked up at him, hesitated, and then tried to get his

Eyes Wide Open

attention without alerting the rest of us. When he glanced at her she leaned closer and discreetly touched her upper lip.

"You've got something stuck in your mustache," she whispered.

His face reddened and he immediately began brushing at his mustache trying to dislodge whatever it was that had attracted her attention. The rest of us paused to watch as Mom sat back, her expression lit with smug self-satisfaction as she sang out a gleeful "April Fools". Dad just smiled and shook his head.

"Now you know you're really part of the family," I laughed.

I haven't tried playing an April Fools joke in ages. It's just not the same without my Mom's unbridled enthusiasm. I made an attempt this year just for old times' sake. I pulled out our binoculars to peer out across the fields outside our kitchen windows.

"I think that's a coyote out there," I announced.

I kept squinting into the binoculars and I heard Bev take two quick steps toward me before he stopped abruptly and turned back to the stove where he was making breakfast.

"I doubt it," he replied.

Eyes Wide Open

He was onto me and I couldn't keep my face straight for one more second. I guess I've lost my touch. It's just as well. We have a better reason to remember April 1st anyway. It was on that day in 1980 that we got engaged.

Eyes Wide Open

A Whole New World

My mother was christened Vjekoslava Godinic when she was born but the family called her Slavica. Her father, my grandpa Ivan Godinic, left their home in Odra near Zagreb in Yugoslavia and travelled to Halifax by ship back in 1930. He planned to settle here in Ontario and earn enough money to pay for passage for his wife and daughter to eventually join him. My mother was only 6 months old when he departed. She wasn't to see him again until she was 10. Times were hard in Canada back then and it was 1939 before he was able to save the money necessary to purchase tickets for his family.

Mom always insisted that she and my grandma, Mariya Godinic travelled to North America on the last voyage that the Queen Mary made before the onset of World War II. If that was the case, she and her mother would have travelled by train from Yugoslavia to the port city of Cherbourg to embark on their long voyage. Neither of them spoke a word of English or French and I can only imagine how stressful it would have been for them trying to make their way in totally unfamiliar territory.

The huge ship was a strange and intimidating world and they spent the first few days hidden away in their cabin subsisting on what was left of the food that her mother had brought along in the capacious bag that she carried with her at all times. Eventually, hunger forced them to venture out and they somehow found their way to the dining room. Mother and daughter sat in uncomfortable silence looking

Eyes Wide Open

around at what other people were eating and drinking. A waiter brought them a menu but they just stared at the unfamiliar words in helpless indecision. Finally, my grandma, who was only twenty seven years old at the time, simply pointed at random to something on the page and shrugged at her daughter as if to say we'll hope for the best. It wasn't long before the waiter returned bearing a tray containing a teapot and cups and saucers along with milk, sugar and a small dish containing freshly cut wedges of lemon. He set it all before them and retreated with the empty tray.

Slavica couldn't conceal her disappointment. The man hadn't brought any food other than lemons and he hadn't even brought any whiskey to flavor the tea. At home they'd always flavored their tea with a splash of whiskey. It was considered normal even for children. She'd never had it any other way. Her mother hushed her with a soft-spoken word and reached into the bag resting at her feet. She pulled out her own bottle of whiskey and proceeded to add a tiny measure to both cups before pouring the tea.

She'd just set the bottle on the table when the waiter came hurrying across the room in a state of obvious agitation. He kept pointing at the bottle and shaking his head but she could make nothing of the torrent of words flowing from his mouth. He snatched the offending bottle from the table and Mariya, thinking he was about to make off with it, jumped up and took hold of it herself. For a moment they stood poised, gripping the bottle between them and staring into each other's eyes in a contest of wills.

Eyes Wide Open

The waiter glanced nervously at the other diners. He must have been conscious that they were making a scene and he decided on a new tactic. By using hand signals he finally managed to convey the idea that he wanted her to put the bottle away and that she shouldn't have taken it out in the dining room. Of course she couldn't understand his objections but she did get the gist of his message. The bottle was returned to the depths of her bag and she and my mother hurriedly finished their tea before making their escape.

They might never have summoned the nerve to return to the dining room if not for the kindness of a stranger. My mother remembers him as a large man in a fur coat. He was Russian but he spoke several languages and he took pity on the two of them. He made it his responsibility to help them and the rest of the voyage passed uneventfully. They would have landed in New York City and then made the rest of the journey into Canada by train.

That trip into Northern Ontario must have felt like an odyssey into the wilderness. The man who met them at the station was a virtual stranger to my mother. He was her father but she had no memory of him and it was as if she was meeting him for the very first time. Everything was strange and different. Children are resilient though. She would have to embrace this new life with all its challenges and make the best of it.

She went to school determined to begin by learning a whole new language. On her very first day one of the other children gave her the English name Gloria when the

Eyes Wide Open

teacher couldn't pronounce her name properly. She became Gloria for the rest of her life even though she discovered years later that her name should have been translated to Sylvia. She learned quickly and eventually was able to speak not only English, but French as well.

She never did lose her accent though. I recently came across one of her hand written recipes for Mikrovave Chicken and I could almost hear her voice even though she's been gone for many years. It made me smile. Young Vjekoslava Godinic definitely made her mark in the new world she found herself a part of.

Eyes Wide Open

Right Between the Eyes

Back in the early 30's my Dad was one of many brothers and sisters living on the family farm near Noelville in Northern Ontario. They kept a few cows and pigs and a henhouse full of chickens. When a litter of pigs was born they were kept until they reached 200 pounds or so before they were sold for meat. It was customary to keep one or two back to be raised for the family larder. Whenever one of the brood sows had outlived her usefulness she would also be sacrificed to the butcher's knife and replaced by a younger animal.

They did all their own butchering right there on the farm. It wasn't a pleasant job but it was necessary and Grandpa Landry wasn't one to shrink from doing what was necessary.

They had one particular sow that they kept for a number of years and every year that pig just got bigger and bigger. Eventually she became the talk of the whole county. Grandpa guessed that she must weigh close to 600 pounds. She measured nearly six feet from snout to tail so she was longer than he was tall. No one had ever seen such an enormous pig. She began to resemble a small hippopotamus and people dropped in to visit just so they could catch a glimpse of her.

One crisp fall morning Grandpa announced that the Day of Reckoning for the old sow had finally come. The children, my Dad included, were keen to see how it would

Eyes Wide Open

be accomplished. The time honored and accepted method of execution was to use the blunt side of a long handled axe rather than a rifle. It was quick and clean and actually quite humane. No need to waste a bullet when one solid blow between the eyes with the heavy axe would drop a pig in its tracks and it would be stone cold dead before hitting the ground. Grandpa was confident that it would work even on a sow of such monumental proportions.

In due course the pig was lured into the shed with a bucket of mash and chained to the centre support post where she stood in sleepy indifference, occasionally shifting her colossal bulk from side to side with her belly nearly brushing the floorboards. Grandpa ordered all the children out and went for the axe. Undeterred, they scrambled up onto the flat roof which was made up of boards that had weathered and shrunk leaving cracks large enough to offer a convenient view of the dim interior. They were perched there like a flock of upended birds, eyes pressed to the boards and rumps in the air when Grandpa returned and entered the shed.

He stood there for a moment hefting the familiar weight of the axe in his hands and taking careful aim. One mighty swing of that axe and his blow landed right on target with a heavy "thunk" that shook the rafters. The sow, however, did not drop down dead as she was meant to do. What would have killed a lesser animal barely seemed to make an impression on her obviously thick skull. She merely let out a squeal of startled outrage and gave her massive head a shake as though to clear it. This was unheard of. There was a collective groan from the children

Eyes Wide Open

watching and Grandpa scowled at the pig as though she were somehow at fault.

He wound up to take a second swing at her and this time he struck her between the eyes with such force that his feet actually left the ground. It didn't even bring her to her knees but it did destroy whatever indifference she'd started out with. She exploded into action, her squeals and grunts deafening in the enclosed space as she thrashed about in her panicked efforts to get away from her attacker. Grandpa jumped clear just in time and ran for the house to fetch his rifle. This was no time to begrudge the bullet he would need to bring the old sow down. The children were frozen into wide-eyed immobility at the terrible drama unfolding below.

Their breathless silence changed to assorted cries of alarm when moments later, the sow made a break for the open door. The chain that held her lashed to the support post proved to be no great obstacle to her freedom. It was never meant to withstand the frantic heaving of a 600 pound behemoth. The post gave way with a loud splintering crack and when it caught in the doorway she pulled part of the wall down as well. In moments the whole shed came down with Dad and the rest of his siblings landing in a tangled heap amidst the rubble.

Grandpa caught up to the runaway pig and finally did her in with the rifle before she got too far. The post and assorted lumber she was dragging behind her slowed her down a bit. He didn't try to shoot her between the eyes....the bullet probably would have bounced off. The shed was a total write-off but apart from a few scrapes and bruises the children emerged very nearly unscathed. This particular job had turned out to be more than unpleasant. It was downright perilous but not one of them would have missed it for the world. My Dad was still telling the story 50 years later.

Eyes Wide Open

The Pitter Patter of Tiny Feet

Bev has always been an extremely light sleeper. The slightest sound that is out of place is enough to wake him. I've known him to get up in the middle of the night because the pump that filled the water troughs in the pasture next to our house failed to cut off as it should. Over the years I learned that no matter how carefully I moved it was impossible for me to get in or out of the bed without alerting him.

He could be snoring heavily only seconds before I'd begin to inch my way out from under the covers in a stealthy attempt to get to the bathroom without spoiling his night's sleep. Inevitably, some whisper of sound would betray me before I could manage to get very far and the snores would come to an abrupt stop. I would freeze and hold my breath hoping that he was simply shifting position until I'd see him reach out to check the time on the bedside clock and hear his muffled voice asking if I was okay. Impossible.

That's why we had serious doubts about the wisdom of acceding to our middle son, Jason's request to have a hamster as a pet. Hamsters are notoriously active during the middle watches of the night and we had visions of Bev never getting a full night's rest again. Still, there were many factors to be considered on the plus side. Jason had a special fondness for small animals and this one could live out its entire life in his bedroom where the rest of us needn't worry about having it underfoot. It seemed much less

Eyes Wide Open

intrusive than a larger pet would have been. Jason was ecstatic when we finally agreed.

He found an oversized birdcage in a garage sale and insisted that he could make it work for his soon to arrive pet. It was tall enough for him to redesign it with three levels which he proceeded to construct with plastic coated wire mesh and ramps leading from one level to the next. The results of his efforts looked like a veritable three story townhouse for up and coming rodents complete with a basement bedroom, middle floor dining area, and a recreation facility in the attic. It boasted air conditioning and spectacular views on all sides. All it needed was a tenant and we duly made the trip to our local pet store to bring home the hamster of Jason's choice. That's how Cookie came to live in the boys' bedroom the summer Jason was 10.

You wouldn't imagine that a hamster would have much in the way of personality but Cookie was unique in that respect. He showed signs of being exceptionally clever and resourceful, not to mention determined. One night at about 3 am I woke up to find Bev down on the floor beside our bed on his hands and knees. I sat up, blinking in the darkness, thinking something must be very far wrong. Perhaps he was taken with some sudden and mysterious illness.

"What's going on? Are you all right?"

Eyes Wide Open

He raised his head to peek at me over the edge of the mattress. "Jason's hamster is loose. I heard it a minute ago," he whispered.

I have to admit I had my doubts. Our room is carpeted and Cookie only weighed about three ounces. It seemed far fetched to think that even Bev could have heard him walking across our bedroom floor in the middle of the night. Then again, Bev specializes in the impossible when it comes to nocturnal noises. I should have remembered that. As it turns out he was right. A diligent search with all the lights turned on revealed the fact that Cookie had indeed escaped and was in the process of transferring as much food as he could carry in his chubby cheeks to a spot in our closet that he had staked out as a getaway retreat.

The fact that he'd been able to get out of his cage at all was a remarkable accomplishment in itself. The only point of egress was a trapdoor in the roof of the contraption that opened outward. He would have had to climb up the side and then hang from the wire ceiling by his front paws at which point he would have to work his way across to the door with his body dangling beneath him. Once there, he'd have to use his head to unlatch the door and push it up enough to allow him to climb out to freedom. We watched in fascination as he proceeded to do just that the moment we'd returned him to his rightful place.

Cookie made a somewhat ungainly acrobat. His technique wouldn't have won him any prizes for style but it was effective. We had to laugh at how absurd he looked with his fat little body swinging to and fro as he reached for

Eyes Wide Open

his next hold on the precarious journey across the ceiling of his cage. Jason was inordinately proud of his pet's unexpected talent but we made it clear that something would have to be done to improve the security on that trapdoor. It turned out that not even a padlock fashioned from a twist tie could offer much hindrance to our furry Houdini.

In the end a massive Funk and Wagnel's Dictionary provided the solution we were looking for. With that weighty tome resting on top of the trapdoor it would take more than a three ounce hamster to push it open.

There would be no more night time visits to our closet and Bev could rest easy knowing that he wouldn't be disturbed in his slumbers by the faint pitter patter of tiny hamster feet. It made me realize that my own efforts to sneak in or out undetected were utterly pointless. I might as well have been wearing bells and whistling Dixie for all the good it would do.

Eyes Wide Open

Home Again and Still Afloat

It was the summer of 1981 and the fishing was good in the French River district in Northern Ontario. When my Uncle Pat and Aunt Lilianne offered to take us on a weekend fishing trip we jumped at the chance. Bev and I had only been married a few months and it seemed like a perfect opportunity for one of those family bonding times. My Mom and Dad were planning on coming along and in a burst of happy inspiration we invited my brand new parents-in-law to join us. That meant there would be eight of us and we would have to do some fancy planning in the logistics department to make it all happen.

Uncle Pat was an experienced guide and he meant to take us down the French River to its outlet in Georgian Bay. We could set up camp on one of the islands there and he was confident that we would have no trouble catching our quota of pickerel in such choice fishing grounds. He offered to take Bev's parents in his own boat along with Aunt Lilianne and most of the supplies.

Mom and Dad had a 16 foot aluminum canoe with a little 3 hp gas motor on the back and Bev borrowed a 14 foot aluminum boat and a motor from a friend for the two of us. The weather was perfect and our spirits were high as we set out from the dock at the marina with our little fleet. Life just couldn't get any better.

There was one point on the journey that offered something of a challenge. The river split into two rocky

Eyes Wide Open

channels and the currents were tricky. One channel was navigable if you knew what you were doing. The other was too dangerous to attempt with a boat. We pulled in to shore and disembarked to walk along the rocks to the lower end of the fast water. Uncle Pat planned to take the boats through one at a time and meet us there.

Naturally, my Dad insisted on taking his own boat through. He would follow closely and didn't expect to have any trouble. Mom didn't even bother to get out. Her confidence wasn't misplaced and the whole transit was accomplished without a hitch. She looked a little smug as she sat there waiting with a smile on her face while the rest of us sorted ourselves out and climbed back aboard to continue down the river.

In due time, we arrived at our destination and chose a likely spot to pitch the tents and establish our camp. The fishing was all we could have hoped for and we feasted on fresh pickerel the whole time we were there. Not even sleeping on the ground could dampen our enthusiasm. We were all a little sorry to see the weekend come to a close when the time came to pack up and head home.

By the time we reached the spot where the river divided I was glad of the chance to get out and stretch my legs. Uncle Pat proceeded to take the first of the boats up through the channel and the rest of us started walking. Mom and Dad, predictably, didn't wait for his return but decided to head up on their own. The first intimation that something was wrong came when we saw my uncle running

Eyes Wide Open

along the rocks waving his arms above his head and shouting.

"Nooo! That's the wrong way!" He turned to us as we scrambled to join him, his alarm all too evident in his clenched fists and tight face. "They're in the wrong channel."

Of course, by that time Dad was well aware of the mistake he'd made. Unfortunately it is quite impossible to turn a 16 foot canoe around once you're caught in a tight place. He had no choice but to go forward and hope that his little motor would be up to the challenge. It was a wild ride with Mom clutching both sides of the canoe in a white-knuckled grip while the churning water tossed them around and threatened to swamp them at any second.

One quick glance at my Dad's grim face was enough to cause her to swallow the scream that was threatening to erupt at any moment. She didn't dare distract him. His blue eyes glittered with a look of fierce determination and his mouth was set in a thin line as he worked to keep them from capsizing in their struggle against the current.

The tension on shore was palpable as we held our breath watching the drama unfold. My uncle was practically jumping up and down as he alternated between muttered curses and shouts of encouragement. It was with profound and heartfelt relief that we saw them emerge from the upper end of the channel, drenched but still afloat.

Eyes Wide Open

We met them at the shore with cheers and many a "Thank God you're safe!" Gone was the look of smug satisfaction that Mom had sported on the trip downriver. She looked decidedly pale.

Mom summed up that unforgettable fishing trip where the ensuing stories had nothing to do with the size of the fish we caught.

"I think I may have peed my pants," she croaked.

Eyes Wide Open

Painful Lessons

One of the things Bev loved about growing up on a farm was the freedom he had to roam over the expanse of their 150 acres when the work was done. Our own children loved to visit the farm where he grew up for the very same reason. The rolling hills and sun kissed fields offered endless possibilities for adventure. There was a stream at the back of one of the farthest fields and close on its banks was a stack of cedar rails left over from the dismantling of a rail fence.

We called it the teepee because that's what it resembled with the rails all standing on end and leaning together at their apex to form a rough circle. It was the perfect destination on the day when Jason and Lauren decided to hike to the back of the farm to pass the time while their older brother, Daniel, was away with the men getting a load of wood. I wasn't worried about letting them go off on their own. Our dog, Brownie, would stay with them and there was nothing dangerous out there anyway…. or at least that's what I thought.

I might have been a little less complacent if I'd known that the first thing they would attempt to do on reaching the teepee was to climb it. I must have forgotten my own childhood and the irresistible power of those three little words "I dare you". It was no surprise that Jason managed to reach the top of the stack but Lauren, not to be outdone, also managed to pull herself up the steeply tilted rails. Brownie was intent on her own pursuits. Her keen

Eyes Wide Open

sense of smell had picked up the scent of some creature hidden away inside the teepee and she was busily nosing around its base looking for some way to get in. She eventually found what she was looking for and immediately squeezed herself into the small opening in an excited attempt to reach whatever animal had its den in there.

The children looked at each other in considerable alarm when her barking changed to yelps of pain and there was a frantic scrabbling that set the whole stack of rails to trembling. The animal she'd cornered in the teepee turned out to be a porcupine and the encounter was an agonizing lesson for Brownie. She managed to get herself turned around in that small space but that just meant that she got hit both front and back. By the time she emerged she was fairly bristling with quills from one end to the other.

Jason had climbed down by then and he could see for himself what had happened. He didn't know much about porcupine quills and he was convinced that if Brownie brushed up against him those spiny darts would stick into him as well. There was only one thing to do….run.

"You better get down," he shouted over his shoulder to Lauren who was still up on the teepee. "Porcupines can climb trees!"

With that parting bit of sage advice he lit out for the house as fast as his legs could carry him. Much to his consternation, Brownie tore off after him and no matter how fast he ran she was never more than a few steps behind him.

Eyes Wide Open

We could hear him screaming long before he appeared in the yard, feet flying and arms pumping wildly with the dog racing at his heels. I couldn't believe he'd run all that way without stopping or slowing down and I wasn't too happy that he'd left his sister back there by herself. Then again, under the circumstances I could see that he felt he'd had no choice.

He was only too happy to go back for her once we had Brownie firmly in hand and there was no further danger of her touching him with the formidable array of quills sticking out of her. As it happens Lauren was already well on her way back to the house by the time he reached her. Jason's warning about tree climbing porcupines was a good incentive not to dally anywhere near the teepee.

Poor Brownie was in terrible pain. Even her eyelids were covered in quills. Bev's sister and I donned heavy gloves and worked together to hold her securely so that she wouldn't drive any of them deeper in her efforts to brush them off. Jason and Lauren, newly returned, kept their distance but watched in wide-eyed silence as we used pliers to try to pull out the quills nearest her eyes. It wasn't working very well. We couldn't do it without hurting her and she kept snapping at the pliers.

In the end we made a quick phone call and bundled her off to the vet in town. He gave her an anesthetic and was able to extract the quills while she slept. He removed over a hundred of them and we still have some of them in a plastic bottle to remind us of that day.

Eyes Wide Open

The children were a little subdued for the next few days as Brownie recovered but it wasn't long before they were back to their usual rambunctious selves…a little older and a little wiser perhaps. Nothing could slow them down for long. At least Brownie learned not to tangle with porcupines. Jason and Lauren drew their own conclusions.

"When in doubt…run!"

You can't argue with that.

Eyes Wide Open

The Pocket Knife

My Dad never had much formal schooling when he was a child. He did attend a small one room schoolhouse in his early years in Northern Ontario for long enough to master the basics. When he was just going into Grade 4, his family moved to a cabin back in the woods and my Grandma Landry carried on with teaching the children their lessons at home. Eventually they moved back to a farm that was close enough to the school for them to join the other children but the teacher refused to recognize the work that had been done at home and Dad was told he would have to repeat the grade. It was to be the last grade he completed before he left school for good to work in the lumber camps with his father and older brother. In the meantime, he was placed back with the younger students and that was a serious blow to his pride.

Perhaps that explains why he felt the need to put on a little extra swagger when he was out in the schoolyard during the lunch break one frosty day in January. It just so happened that he was carrying a brand new pocket knife. It was his most treasured possession and he brought it out to carve himself a whistle from a twig he stripped from a tree in the yard. The other boys cast envious glances at that shiny new knife as they gathered around him to watch. He even consented to let one of them hold it for a moment before the bell rang to call them back to their desks.

That was the beginning. That very afternoon one of the boys tried to buy the pocket knife from him. He offered

Eyes Wide Open

him a whole nickel but Dad was adamant that the knife was not for sale. He didn't reckon on how determined that boy was. He simply refused to accept "no" as a final answer. He was convinced that if he kept at it long enough and tried every incentive he could think of Dad would eventually give in.

Over the next few days his dogged persistence became a form of exquisite torture to Dad. It seemed that no matter where he went he couldn't escape that wheedling voice. Telling the boy to quit did no good at all and attempts at ignoring him failed utterly. He almost regretted ever bringing the knife to school in the first place but what was the use of having a treasure if you couldn't show it off from time to time.

He couldn't even walk home in peace with his young schoolmate trailing along behind him offering in his most coaxing tones to do whatever Dad asked if only he would give up his pocketknife. Finally, in a fit of exasperation, Dad stopped in the middle of the snowy road and turned to his tormenter who skidded to an eager halt beside him.

"So you'll do whatever I say will you?" he shouted. "Well then…eat that!" He pointed to a pile of horse droppings that lay frozen on the ground and then stood scowling his most formidable scowl with his arms folded across his chest as he waited.

Now horse droppings, sometimes known as "road apples", could hardly be termed an appetizing prospect even

Eyes Wide Open

in a frozen state. Dad was fairly confident that his demand would be the end of it once and for all. It wasn't his fault that he seriously underestimated the strength of the boy's resolve. He must have wanted that pocketknife in the worst way because he only hesitated for a moment.

He snatched up one of the hard brown lumps, screwed his eyes tightly shut and sank his teeth into it before Dad could even think about saying he changed his mind. It was inevitable that a fight would ensue. The boy loudly insisted that he had done what was asked and the knife was his while Dad just as loudly proclaimed that one bite was not the same as eating, especially since he'd meant for him to eat the whole pile. There was no way that he was going to hand over his precious knife. What began as a shouting match quickly degenerated to the two of them rolling around on the ground pummeling one another for all they were worth.

In the end, Dad emerged victorious. His shirt was torn and his nose bloodied but the knife still rested where it belonged…in his pocket. He smiled to himself when he thought of how the boy finally cried mercy and promised to give it up for good. "I should have done that in the first place," he thought. The smile slipped a fraction as he pictured the tanning he would get from his mother when she saw the state of his shirt. Ah well, it was worth it.

Eyes Wide Open

Pest Control

     The place that Bev and I call home is a farmhouse out in the country that we've lived in for the past 19 years. The house actually qualifies as a heritage home since it was built over 150 years ago. It's a house that has character as a number of visitors over the years have pointed out. I have to agree that the tall ceilings, deep windowsills and spacious hallway give it a certain flair. The house doesn't belong to us but we've always considered ourselves blessed to have the opportunity to live here. I do have to admit that there are a few quirks that go along with living in a home of such a venerable age. To say that it is well ventilated would be an understatement of gargantuan proportions.

     A number of years ago a study was done to determine the efficiency of the heating systems in the various houses managed by the university. On the appointed day a massive fan was installed and sealed into our open front door. It was designed to suck air out of the house to lower the air pressure inside and determine how airtight it might be. It was an impossible task because as fast as the air was sucked out it was replaced by a constant and substantial inflow from nearly every direction. Curtains billowed in front of tightly shut windows while doors trembled on their hinges in the breeze.

     To open any one of the kitchen cupboards that sat against an outside wall was to be blasted by a veritable windstorm blowing out from among the canned goods. Even the plaster walls seemed to be oozing air. In the end

Eyes Wide Open

they gave it up and concluded that at the very least we didn't need to worry about being asphyxiated in our sleep by carbon monoxide poisoning. We resigned ourselves to wrapping up in comforters to watch television and occasionally wearing knee high felt boot liners around the house in winter.

The other problem with living in a house with more than its fair share of cracks and holes is that we have to deal with the pests that manage to find their way inside. Every spring and fall we have an influx of cluster flies that gives me a deep appreciation for what the Egyptians must have endured during the plagues of the Exodus. The first snowfall generally heralds the entrance of a few field mice looking to get in out of the cold and occasionally we get a visitor of a more alarming sort.

Our daughter, Lauren, found herself stirring out of a restless sleep in the middle hours of a warm summer night the year she was 12 years old. She lay in bed wondering what could have wakened her, absently noting that the rhythmic whirring of the ceiling fan sounded a lot louder than it ought to. Her eyes snapped open completely when she belatedly remembered that there was no ceiling fan in her room. Something was flying in circles in the darkness above her head! What else could it be but a bat? She snatched the covers up over her head and called out softly in an attempt to attract our attention without alerting the winged intruder to her presence.

Back in our room, Bev raised himself up on one elbow and cocked his head to listen.

Eyes Wide Open

"What's wrong," I muttered.

He was already getting out of bed and pulling on some clothes. "I heard someone calling Daddy," he whispered. "It had to be Lauren. I'll just go check on her."

In the meantime, Lauren was convinced that no one could have heard her feeble cry. She decided she couldn't stay where she was so she gently rolled out from under the covers and off the edge of her bed to a prone position on the carpet. Bats were supposed to have excellent radar but she wasn't about to stand up and risk a collision. She began a slow torturous crawl along the floor while the whirring continued unabated somewhere near the ceiling above her. She'd almost reached the door when Bev arrived and pushed it open. He looked down in astonishment as she scooted past his ankles and pulled the door shut behind her.

"There's a bat flying around in there," she gasped.

Bev grabbed a towel from the bathroom and stepped through the door into Lauren's room closing it firmly behind him before flicking the light switch on. Sure enough, there was a bat flying circles around the room at just above head height. Bev stood watching long enough to see that its flight path never seemed to vary. He simply stepped in front of it on one of its crazy circuits and caught it in the folds of the towel. From there it was easy enough to carry it outside and set it free…a classic catch and release.

Eyes Wide Open

Lauren was mightily relieved. She returned to her bed surrounded by the blessed sounds of silence. Still, she spent the rest of the night with her lights on.

Eyes Wide Open

Galaxy Gaffe

My husband Bev and I went to the movies last night. I love movies as did my mother before me. My dad was a different kettle of fish. I think he viewed the dimming of the lights as his cue to settle in for a good long nap. Even so, he wouldn't dream of not coming along if we decided to head for the theater. He managed to sleep blissfully through the entire screening of the first Star Wars movie when it came out years ago. Completely oblivious to the roar of turbolasers and blaster fire, he sat with his chin resting on his chest and dreamed his way right through to the final credits.

As he got older they stopped going to the movies. I think he was finding the seats too uncomfortable to provide for a good two hour snooze. I finally convinced them that the new Galaxy Cinemas had seats to rival his lazy boy at home and we all went to see the Italian Job when it came out. True to form, he was a goner before the opening heist was even under way. We glanced over at his awkward slouch and the gentle rise and fall of his chest as he breathed. At least he wasn't snoring. My mother and I shook our heads and smiled at each other in mild exasperation before settling back to watch the action on the screen.

It was about three fourths of the way through the movie, right during the famous car chase scene with the three Austin Minis barreling through the storm drain, motorcycles hot on their tails, when my dad suddenly

Eyes Wide Open

stirred and sat up straighter. He was a bit hard of hearing so the entire audience was privy to his question as his voice rang out into a momentary hush.

"So…what's this movie about anyway?"

Embarrassing? Absolutely! Yet it remains one of my favorite movie memories to this day. My dad is gone now but every time I sit in the Galaxy or watch my copy of the Italian Job I feel a smile tugging at the corners of my mouth. I imagine him there beside me and I miss him, gaffes and all.

Eyes Wide Open

Too Close For Comfort

Hunting larger game with my Dad was not for the faint of heart. Those were the days before modern technology simplified life. No GPS, ATV or hand held radio for him. He had only his own two feet and an uncanny sense of direction to depend on. He did occasionally take someone along with him but more often than not it was a solitary venture. He preferred to hunt alone.

He would head off on foot into the bush in Northern Ontario to look for signs of the deer or moose that he was after. Once he found tracks and knew which direction they were heading, he would take some time to study the terrain. He was quite skilled at predicting the path they were likely to take and he would set off on a route that would take him around in a wide circle to get in front of them. Then he could pick a spot that would put him downwind and in a perfect position to take a shot when the time came. Of course, all that tracking and circling meant that he often covered a lot of distance on a hunt. Anyone tagging along was taking the risk that they might find themselves trudging through 20 miles of forest and swamps before the day was done.

Dad was good at what he did so he seldom failed to bring home his prey. Once the animal was shot the real work began. If it was a deer he would shoulder the whole carcass after it was gutted and begin the long trek back to the road. If it was a moose things got a little more

Eyes Wide Open

complicated. A moose is far too large to drag through the woods so it would have to be butchered on site. One man couldn't hope to carry it all.

Help would be needed in order to retrieve it and that meant hiking back to civilization to round up reinforcements. With a little luck there would be some relative or friend who was willing to lend a hand in exchange for a share of the meat. If no one was available he would head back on his own with a huge pack he kept for the purpose and used often. It would hold about 200 pounds and he would load it up with the choicest cuts and leave the rest for scavengers. Bushwhacking with a 200 pound pack on your back for any distance can take the stuffing out of even the strongest of men but Dad did it when he had to. It was all part of the experience.

One year he was out after deer with his 300 Savage lever action rifle. He'd been walking for some time and was caught completely by surprise when a moose rose to its feet almost directly in front of him. It was a cow and his reaction was instinctive. He lifted the rifle to his shoulder and fired before he had time to think about it.

The 300 is shorter and lighter than the gun he normally would have carried to hunt moose but it was a good clean shot and she went down like a stone. He'd only taken a few steps toward her when a crashing in the brush some distance behind him brought him up short. He swung around in alarm to see a huge bull moose snorting and shaking his massive antlered head at the puny man that stood between him and the cow he'd been approaching.

Eyes Wide Open

When the animal charged Dad stood his ground and fired. He fired again and again until he'd used all 5 of the shots that remained in his gun after the one that brought the cow down. The big bull not only kept coming, it didn't even slow down. I don't know if Dad's life flashed before his eyes in that moment but it well might have. He took a quick step back and stumbled, the now empty and useless gun dangling from one hand. He fell onto his back and lay there helpless as the moose, confused by the sudden move, skidded to a stop and stood panting over him.

He was close…so close that Dad could have reached up and touched his lowered head. There was blood streaming from the broad chest where his shots had found a mark but it was obvious that with the lighter rifle he had failed to pierce anything vital. He held his breath and waited through ten long agonizing seconds before the moose turned aside and trotted off through the trees. He was lucky to be alive. As it was, he didn't even get stepped on.

"I thought I was a goner," he later confided. "It was a little too close for comfort."

Eyes Wide Open

The Runt of the Flock

Spring is the time of year for babies to be born…at least in the animal world. The woods and fields are bursting with new life. A trip to the barn yields its own reward with the sight of gangly new calves or lambs frisking in the yard whenever they're not suckling, their tails twitching madly in their eagerness. There is something infinitely appealing about baby animals. Perhaps it is their very newness and vulnerability that pulls at our heartstrings. Whatever the reason, they can be irresistible.

That's why I jumped at the chance for a visit to the farm where Bev owned a quarter share in a flock of 100 angora goats back in the spring of 1980 when we were newly engaged. I met him at his apartment after work and we drove out to the farm together. The place would be just about exploding with new babies and I could hardly wait.

Angora goats are raised for their wool like sheep. The adult animals produce mohair but it is the first fleece of the young animals that produces the soft angora wool that we prize so much. The kids were even smaller than new lambs and covered in the finest silky white curls…adorable! I stood at the gate and watched, completely captivated.

"What's wrong with that one?" I took hold of Bev's coat sleeve and pointed to a tiny kid I'd spotted off to one side. "I think it's limping," I observed, my brow furrowing with concern.

Eyes Wide Open

"Yeah," Bev replied. "She was born a couple of weeks before the rest and I think she was a bit premature. Then she got stepped on so one of her front legs got damaged. It's not broken but you can see how she doesn't put much weight on it. She doesn't feed well and so she hasn't been growing. The others are all bigger than her even though they were born later."

"What's going to happen to her?" I wondered.

He gave a shrug and shook his head. "We don't expect her to survive," he admitted.

I could feel myself going all maternal all of a sudden. It must have something to do with how God wired the female of the species. I just couldn't let it go at that.

"Couldn't we take her out of there?" I asked. "We could take her down to your parents' farm in Markdale and give her to your little sisters as a pet." It seemed reasonable enough.

"That's not a bad idea," Bev admitted. "She might do a lot better with all the attention they'd give her."

It was a long drive to Bev's family home and we decided to go the very next day. In the end we hashed out a plan that involved me taking the baby goat home to my apartment for the night so we could get an early start. I somehow convinced my part time farmer fiancé that we ought to give her a bath. Warm water in a laundry tub, one bottle of baby shampoo and we were both up to our elbows

Eyes Wide Open

in lather as we worked her over. I don't know what she thought of the proceedings but the end result was worth it. Her curls felt unbelievably soft and she smelled like a Johnson and Johnson baby.

    I bundled her into my car in a cardboard box and headed back into town with Bev's promise to be there first thing in the morning. Till then I would be on my own. I made sure the coast was clear before I smuggled her up the stairs to my apartment. Once there I built a barricade to block off one corner of the kitchen, laid a sheet of plastic on the floor and tossed in the straw from her box. She didn't seem too impressed. I discovered that a baby goat can make an incredible amount of noise when they're upset. It sounded almost like a human baby crying and I began to worry about what my landlord would think was going on upstairs.

    I thought she might be lonely for the other goats so I unscrewed the full length mirror from my bedroom door and leaned it against the wall in her corner. Perhaps if she saw her image in the mirror she could be fooled into thinking she wasn't alone. It seemed to work for the first little while but it didn't take long for her to set up her lament all over again.

    Finally, in desperation, I put her back in the box and set it right next to my bed. If I slept with one arm dangling over the side so that my hand rested in the box with her she seemed to settle down. I guess she needed contact with something warm and alive and in the absence of her mother, my hand would do. By morning I was convinced of the

Eyes Wide Open

wisdom of not keeping farm animals in apartments and it was with considerable relief that I saw Bev's truck pull up to the curb.

The five hour trip went without incident and the girls were absolutely delighted with the surprise we brought them. The runt of the flock didn't die after all. With all the TLC she got it wasn't long before she began to thrive and grow. Eventually, Bev's sisters were able to start a flock of their own with our little runt as the matriarch. Instead of survival of the fittest it was survival of the most loved.

Eyes Wide Open

It Feels Real

My Mom was just about the age that I am now the first time she had breast cancer. She must have had the lump for some time before she finally decided to go to a doctor about it. I suppose she hoped that it would go away if she left it alone. Things might have turned out differently if she'd had some of the information available to women today along with the breast screening programs now in place to help with early detection. As it was, she went straight from the Doctor's office to the hospital where she was hurriedly admitted. Less than 48 hours later she woke from anesthetic having had a radical mastectomy.

I won't say she had an easy time of it. She did raise an eyebrow or two on the hospital ward when she declared that she was as good with one boob as she'd ever been with two. Cancer terrified her and she was so relieved to have it gone that her breast seemed a small price to pay. She did not grieve its loss though it would have been understandable if she had.

The Doctors recommended a whole series of radiation treatments. There were very few side effects apart from a lingering shadow of fear that the cancer would return one day. It tended to creep to the surface every time she had to go for a checkup.

Her wacky sense of humor tipped the scales in her favor over the years that followed. Laughter seemed to give her strength. In time she recovered enough from that

Eyes Wide Open

initial surgery to be measured and fitted for a prosthesis that could be worn in a specially made bra. She was as delighted with her new "falsie" as a child on Christmas morning. The first time she tried it on she stood before the mirror in her room examining herself critically from every angle.

"You can't even tell the difference," she announced as she peered closely at her reflection. She gave herself a little jiggle to see how it moved and then tried a couple of quick hops. She grinned in satisfaction and came out to show off her newly restored figure to the rest of the family.

"I bet you wouldn't be able to tell which one was which if you didn't know," she insisted.

In fact, much to our embarrassment, she was not averse to issuing that very challenge to anyone who asked about her surgery in the weeks that followed. One poor fellow nearly choked on his coffee at dinner when she blithely asserted to the table at large that "It actually feels real."

He wasn't sure he'd heard correctly but her next words confirmed it.

"Go ahead and give it a poke," she offered with an earnest smile and a nod in his direction.

He hastily swiped a dribble of coffee from his chin and, darting a quick look in my Dad's direction, shook his head vigorously.

Eyes Wide Open

"Why not?" she asked. "It's not me you'll be touching you know. I don't mind."

He glanced at his wife and then back at my Dad but got no help from either of them. They just sat there grinning at his discomfiture. Finally he reached out a tentative finger and gave the proffered breast a gentle prod.

"Not that one," Mom snapped in tones of righteous indignation.

He jerked his hand away nearly toppling his chair in the process while my Mom broke into peals of laughter. The whole table was in an uproar.

"I'm just kidding," she gasped. "I told you it feels real!"

"I guess you got me there," he admitted with a grin of his own as he struggled to regain his composure.

Mom lived another twenty years. Eventually she lost her remaining breast…again to cancer. Her response was not unexpected.

"Well," she shrugged. "Now I won't need to bother with a bra at all. I never liked them anyway."

There's always a bright side if you're willing to look for it.

Eyes Wide Open

****

Dusk has fallen and the day is spent. Tomorrow it will be back to the routines of everyday life and whatever unlooked for adventures await us there. Given the opportunity we'll no doubt make a few of our own.

The shining eagerness I see in the faces around me has a strangely familiar feel. Mom and Dad aren't quite gone after all - something of their spirit remains.

****

"...For the happy heart, life is a continual feast."

Proverbs 15:15 NLT